ANARCHY AND CHRISTIANITY

Anarchy
and
Christianity

JACQUES ELLUL

translated by
Geoffrey W. Bromiley

WILLIAM B. EERDMANS PUBLISHING COMPANY
GRAND RAPIDS, MICHIGAN

Originally published as *Anarchie et Christianisme*
by Atelier de creation libertaire
13, rue Pierre-Blanc, 69001 Lyon, France

Copyright © 1988 by Atelier de creation libertaire

First English edition copyright © 1991 by
Wm. B. Eerdmans Publishing Co.
2140 Oak Industrial Drive N.E., Grand Rapids, Mich. 49505
All rights reserved

Printed in the United States of America

Library of Congress Cataloging-in-Publication Data

Ellul, Jacques.
    [Anarchie et christianisme. English]
    Anarchy and Christianity / Jacques Ellul; translated by
Geoffrey W. Bromiley.
        p.   cm.
    Translation of: Anarchie et christianisme.
    Includes bibliographical references.
    ISBN 978-0-8028-0495-2
    1. Anarchism — Biblical teaching.   2. Bible — Criticism, interpretation,
etc.   3. Christianity and politics.   4. Christianity and international affairs.
I. Title.
BS672.E4413   1991
261.7 — dc20   91-9779
                                                                      CIP

Contents

CONTENTS

Introduction

The question I am posing is the more difficult because fixed opinions have long since been reached on both sides and have never been subjected to the least examination. It is taken for granted that anarchists are hostile to all religions (and Christianity is classified as such). It is also taken for granted that devout Christians abhor anarchy as a source of disorder and a negation of established authority. It is these simplistic and uncontested beliefs that I propose to challenge. But it might be useful to say where I am coming from, as students used to say in 1968. I am a Christian, not by descent but by conversion.

When I was young, I had a horror of fascist movements. I demonstrated against the Fiery Cross on February 10, 1934. Intellectually I was much influenced by Marx. I do not deny that this was less due to intellectual than to family considerations. My father was out of work after the 1929 crisis, and we have to remember what it was like to be unemployed in 1930. There were also individual circumstances. As a student I came into conflict with the police (e.g., during the Jèze strike), and I came to abhor not so much the capitalist system as the state. Nietzsche's description of the state as the coldest of all cold monsters seemed to me to be basic.

Though I liked the analyses of Marx, including his vision of a society in which the state would have withered away, my contacts with communists were poor. They viewed me as a little bourgeois intellectual because I did not show total respect for orders from Moscow, and I regarded them as insignificant because they seemed not to have any true knowledge of the thinking of Marx. They had read the 1848 Manifesto, and that was all. I broke with them completely after the Moscow trials, not in favor of Trotsky, for the Cronstadt sailors and the Makhno government seemed to me to have been truly revolutionary and I could not pardon their suppression, but because I could not believe that Lenin's great companions were traitors, antirevolutionaries, etc. As I saw it, their condemnation was simply another manifestation of the cold monster. I also saw with no great difficulty that there had been a transition from a dictatorship of the proletariat to a dictatorship over the proletariat. I can guarantee that anyone who was willing could see already in 1935 and 1936 what would be denounced twenty years later. Furthermore, nothing remained of the two basic principles of internationalism and pacifism, which ought to have resulted in antinationalism.

My admiration for Marx was also tempered by the following fact. At the same time as I had read Marx I had also read Proudhon, who did not impress me so much but whom I greatly liked, so that I was scandalized by the attitude of Marx to him in their dispute. Finally, what led to me to detest the communists was their conduct during the Spanish Civil War and their horrible assassination of the Barcelona anarchists.

Many things, including contacts at that time with the Spanish anarchists, attracted me to anarchism. But there was one insurmountable obstacle — I was a Christian. I came up against this obstacle all my life. For instance, in 1964 I was attracted by a movement very close to anarchism, that is, situationism. I had very friendly contacts with Guy Debord, and one day I asked him bluntly whether I could join his movement and work with him. He said that he would ask his comrades. Their answer was frank. Since I was a Christian I could not belong to their movement. For my part, I could not renounce my faith. Reconciling the two things was not an easy matter. It was possible to conceive of being both a Christian and a socialist. There had been a Christian socialism for many years, and around 1940 a moderate socialism drew its moral teachings from the Bible. But it hardly seemed possible to go any further. From both angles the incompatibility seemed to be absolute.

I thus embarked on a long spiritual and intellectual quest, not to reconcile the two positions but to see if I was finally schizophrenic. The strange result was that the more I studied and the more I understood seriously the biblical message in its entirety (and not simply the "gentle" gospel of Jesus), the more I came to see how impossible it is to give simple obedience to the state and how there is in the Bible the orientation to a certain anarchism. Naturally, this was a personal view. At this point I parted company with the theology which had formed me, that is, that of Karl Barth, who continued to uphold the validity of political authority. Yet during the last few years I have come across other studies pointing in the same direction, especially in the USA: Murray Bookchin, who freely admits that the origin of Christianity was in anarchist thinking, and Vernard Eller. Nor should I forget a pioneer, Henri Barbusse, who was not a true anarchist, but whose work on Jesus shows clearly that Jesus was not merely a socialist but an anarchist — and I want to stress here that I regard anarchism as the fullest and most serious form of socialism. Slowly then, and on my own, not emotionally but intellectually, I arrived at my present position.

I need to clear up another point before getting down to my subject. What is my purpose in writing these pages? I think it is important to state this in order to prevent any misunderstanding. First, it must be clear that, on the one hand, I have no proselytizing aim. I am not trying to convert anarchists to the Christian faith. This is not simply a matter of honesty. It rests on a biblical basis. For centuries the churches have preached that we must choose between damnation and conversion. With good faith preachers and zealous missionaries have sought conversions at all costs in order to save souls. As I see it, however, this is a mistake. To be sure, there are verses which tell us that if we believe we shall be saved. But a fundamental point here that is often forgotten is that we must not take biblical verses out of the context (the story or argument) to which they belong. My own belief is that the Bible proclaims a universal salvation which God in grace grants to all of us. But what about conversion and faith? That is another matter. It does not relate so much to salvation, in spite of the common view. It is a taking of responsibility. After conversion we are committed to a certain lifestyle and to a certain service that God requires of us. Hence adherence to the Christian faith is not in any sense a privilege in relation to other people but an additional commission, a responsibility, a new work. We are not, then, to engage in proselytizing.

On the other hand, I am not in any way trying to tell Christians that they ought to be anarchists. My point is simply this. Among the political options, if they take a political path, they should not rule out anarchism in advance, for in my view this seems to be the position which in this area is closest to biblical thinking. Naturally, I realize that I have little chance of being heard, for it is not easy in a few years to cast off inveterate secular prejudices. I would also add that my objective cannot be that Christians should regard taking this position as a duty, for again, in spite of the view of many centuries, the Christian faith does not bring us into a world of duty and obligation but into a life of freedom. I myself do not say this but Paul does in many places (e.g., 1 Corinthians).[1]

Third, I am not trying here to reconcile at all costs two forms of thinking and action, two attitudes to life, which I hold. Now that Christianity is no longer dominant in society, it is a stupid mania on the part of Christians to cling to this or that ideology and to abandon that which embarrasses them in Christianity. Thus many Christians turned to Stalinist communism after 1945. They emphasized whatever Christianity has to say about the poor, about social justice, about the attempt to change society, and neglected what they found uncomfortable — the proclamation of the sovereignty of God and of salvation in Jesus Christ. In the 1970s we saw the same tendency in the so-called liberation theologies. In an extreme form a strategy has been found to make possible association with (South American) revolutionary movements. A poor person of any kind is supposedly identical with Jesus Christ. Hence there is no problem. As for the event two thousand years ago, little attention is paid to it. These orientations were broadly preceded by that of rationalistic Protestantism around 1900 with its simple presupposition that since science is always right, and has the truth, then in preserving the Bible and the gospel we must abandon everything that is contrary to science and reason, for example, the possibility that God incarnated himself in a man, along with the miracles, the resurrection, etc.

Finally, in our own time we again find the same attitude of conciliation by abandonment of one part of Christianity,

1. Cf. my *Ethique de la liberté*, 3 vols. (Geneva: Labor et Fides, 1975-1984) (condensed Eng. trans. *Ethics of Freedom* [Grand Rapids: Eerdmans, 1976]), in which I show that freedom is the central truth of the Bible and that the biblical God is above all else the Liberator. As Paul says, it is for liberty that we are freed, and as James says, the perfect law is that of liberty.

but this time in favor of Islam. Christians passionately want understanding with Muslims, and so in conversations (in which I have participated) they insist strongly on the points of agreement, for example, that both religions are mono-theistic and both are religions of the book,[2] etc. No reference is made to the main point of conflict, that is, Jesus Christ. I ask myself why they still call their religion Christianity. Readers are forewarned, then, that I am not trying here to show at all costs a convergence between anarchism and biblical faith. I am arguing for what I take to be the sense of the Bible, which can become for me the true Word of God. I think that in dialogue with those of different views, if we are to be honest, we must be true to ourselves and not veil ourselves or dissimulate or abandon what we think. Thus anarchist readers might find in these pages many statements that seem shocking or ridiculous, but that does not worry me.

What, then, am I trying to do? Simply to erase a great misunderstanding for which Christianity is to blame. There has developed in effect a kind of corpus which practically all Christian groups accept but which has nothing in common with the biblical message, whether in the Hebrew Bible that we call the Old Testament or the Gospels and Epistles of the New Testament. All the churches have scrupulously respected and often supported the state authorities. They have made of conformity a major virtue. They have tolerated social injustices and the exploitation of some people by others, explaining that it is God's will that some should be masters and others servants, and that socioeconomic success is an outward sign of divine blessing. They have thus transformed the free and liberating Word into morality, the most aston-

2. I have shown elsewhere that the biblical God really has nothing in common with Allah. We need to remember that we can read anything we like into the word "God." I have also shown that apart from some names and stories the Bible and the Koran have nothing in common.

ishing thing being that there can be no Christian morality if we truly follow evangelical thinking. The fact is that it is much easier to judge faults according to an established morality than to view people as living wholes and to understand why they act as they do. Finally, all the churches have set up a clergy furnished with knowledge and power, though this is contrary to evangelical thinking, as was initially realized when the clergy were called ministers, *ministerium* being service and the minister a servant of others.

Hence we have to eliminate two thousand years of accumulated Christian errors, or mistaken traditions,[3] and I do not say this as a Protestant accusing Roman Catholics, for we have all been guilty of the same deviations or aberrations. Nor do I want to say that I am the first to take this move or that I have discovered anything. I do not pretend to be able to unveil things hidden from the beginning of the world. The position that I take is not a new one in Christianity. I will first study the biblical foundations for the relation between Christianity and anarchism. I will then take a look at the attitude of Christians in the first three centuries. But what I write is not a sudden resurgence after seventeen centuries of obscurity. There has always been a Christian anarchism. In every century there have been Christians who have discovered the simple biblical truth, whether intellectually, mystically, or socially. They include some great names, for example, Tertullian (at first), Fra Dolcino, Francis of Assisi, Wycliffe, Luther (except for the twofold mistake of putting power back in the hands of the princes and supporting the massacre of rebellious peasants), Lammenais, John Bost, and Charles de Foucauld.

For a detailed study I recommend the excellent work of

3. Some time ago I explained this movement from the Bible to what I call Christianity, with political and economic reasons, etc.; see my *Subversion of Christianity* (Grand Rapids: Eerdmans, 1986).

[7]

Vernard Eller.[4] This brings to light the true character of Anabaptism, which rejects the power of rulers and which is not apolitical, as is usually said, but true anarchy, yet with the nuance that I quote ironically, namely, that the powers that be are a divine scourge sent to punish the wicked. Christians, however, if they act properly and are not wicked, do not need to obey the political authorities but should organize themselves in autonomous communities on the margin of society and government. Even more strictly and strangely, that extraordinary man Christoph Blumhardt formulated a consistently anarchist Christianity toward the end of the 19th century. A pastor and theologian, he joined the extreme left but would not enter into the debate about seizing power. At a Red congress he declared: "I am proud to stand before you as a man; and if politics cannot tolerate a human being as I am, then let politics be damned!" This is the true essence of anarchism: To become a human being, yes, but a politician, never. Blumhardt had to leave the party!

In the middle of the 19th century Blumhardt had been preceded on the anarchist path by Kierkegaard, the father of existentialism, who would not let himself be ensnared by any power. He is despised and rejected today as an individualist. To be sure, he ruthlessly condemned the masses and all authorities, even though they be based on democracy. One of his phrases was that "no mistake or crime is more horrible to God than those committed by power. Why? Because what is official is impersonal, and being impersonal is the greatest insult that can be paid to a person." In many passages Kierkegaard shows himself to be an anarchist, though naturally the term does not occur, since it did not then exist.[5] Finally,

---

4. Eller, *Christian Anarchy* (Grand Rapids: Eerdmans, 1987).
5. See Vernard Eller, *Kierkegaard and Radical Discipleship* (Princeton: Princeton University Press, 1968).

Eller's most convincing proof in my eyes is that Karl Barth, the greatest theologian of the 20th century, was an anarchist before he was a socialist, but favorable to communism, of which he repented. These simple facts show that my studies are not an exception in Christianity.

Alongside the illustrious intellectuals and theologians we should not forget the popular movements, the constant existence of humble people who lived out a faith and truth that were different from those proclaimed by the official churches and that found their source directly in the gospel rather than in a collective movement. These humble witnesses maintained a true and living faith without being persecuted as heretics so long as they caused no scandal. What I am advancing is by no means a rediscovered truth. It has always been upheld, but by a small number of people, mostly anonymous, though their traces remain.[6] They have always been there even though they have constantly been effaced by the official and authoritarian Christianity of church dignitaries. Whenever they succeeded in launching a renewal, the movement that they started on the basis of the gospel and the whole Bible was quickly perverted and reentered the path of official conformity. This happened to the Franciscans after Francis and to the Lutherans after Luther. Externally, then, they did not exist. We see and know only the pomp of the great church, the pontifical encyclicals, the political positions of this or that Protestant authority.

I have very concrete knowledge of this. My wife's father, who was doggedly non-Christian, told me when I tried to explain to him the true message of the gospel that it was I alone who told him this, that he heard it only from me, and that what he heard in the churches was the exact opposite.

6. Cf. the interesting founding of confraternities in the 7th and 8th centuries.

[9]

Now I do not pretend to be the only one to say it. There has been an ongoing faithful subterranean current, but no less invisible than faithful. It is that that is in keeping with the biblical Word. That and not the rest — the pomp, the spectacles, the official declarations, the simple fact of organizing a hierarchy (which Jesus himself plainly did not create), an institutional authority (which the prophets never had), a judicial system (to which true representatives of God never had recourse). These visible things are the sociological and institutional aspect of the church but no more; they are not the church. On the outside, however, they obviously are the church. Hence we cannot judge outsiders when they themselves judge the church. In other words, anarchists are right to reject Christianity. Kierkegaard attacked it more violently than any of them. Here I simply want to sound another note and dispel some misunderstandings. I will not try to justify what is said and done by the official church or the majority of those who are called sociological Christians, that is, those who say that they are Christians (happily in diminishing numbers, for it is they who leave the church in times of crisis) and who behave precisely in a non-Christian way, or who, like the patrons of the church in the 19th century, use certain features of Christianity to increase their power over others.

I. Anarchy from a
Christian Standpoint

1. What Anarchy?

There are different forms of anarchy and different currents in it. I must first say very simply what anarchy I have in view. By anarchy I mean first an absolute rejection of violence. Hence I cannot accept either nihilists or anarchists who choose violence as a means of action. I certainly understand the resort to aggression, to violence. I recall passing the Paris Bourse some twenty years ago and saying to myself that a bomb ought to be placed under that building. It would not destroy capitalism but it would serve as a symbol and a warning. Not knowing anyone who could make a bomb, I took no action!

The resort to violence is explicable, I think, in three situations. First, we have the doctrine of the Russian nihilists that if action is taken systematically to kill those who hold power — the ministers, generals, and police chiefs — in the long run people will be so afraid to take office that the state will be decapitated and easy to pull down. We find something of the same orientation among modern terrorists. But this line of thinking greatly underestimates the ability of powerful organisms, as well as society, to resist and react. Then there is despair when the solidity of the system is seen, when impotence is felt face-to-face with an increasingly conformist society, or an increasingly powerful administration, or an invincible economic system (who can arrest multinationals?), and violence is a kind of cry of despair, an ultimate act by which an effort is made to give public expression to one's disagreement and hatred of the oppression. It is our present despair which is crying aloud (J. Rictus). But it is also the confession that there is no other course of action and no reason to hope.

Finally, there is the offering of a symbol and a sign, to which I have alluded already. A warning is given that society is more fragile than is supposed and that secret forces are at work to undermine it.

No matter what the motivation, however, I am against violence and aggression. I am against it on two levels. The first is simply tactical. We have begun to see that movements of nonviolence, when they are well managed (and this demands strong discipline and good strategy), are much more effective than violent movements (except when a true revolution is unleased). We not only recall the success of Gandhi but nearer home it is also evident that Martin Luther King did much to advance the cause of American Blacks, whereas later movements, for example, the Black Muslims and Black Panthers, which wanted to make quicker headway by using all kinds of violence, not only gained nothing but even lost some of the gains made by King. Similarly, the violent movements in Berlin in 1956, then in Hungary and Czechoslovakia, all failed, but Lech Walesa, by imposing a strict discipline of nonviolence on his union, held his own against the Polish government. One of the sayings of the great union leaders of the years 1900-1910 was this: Strikes, yes, but violence, never. Finally, though this is debatable, the great Zulu chieftain in South Africa, Buthelezi, supports a strategy of total nonviolence as opposed to Mandela (of the Xhosa tribe), and by all accounts he could do infinitely more to end apartheid than will be achieved by the erratic violence (often between blacks) of the African National Congress. An authoritarian government can respond to violence only with violence.

My second reason is obviously a Christian one. Biblically, love is the way, not violence (in spite of the wars recounted in the Hebrew Bible,[1] which I frankly confess to be most embarrassing).[2] Not using violence against those in power does not mean doing nothing. I will have to show that Christianity means a rejection of power and a fight against it. This was completely forgotten during the centuries of the alliance of throne and altar, the more so as the pope became a head of state, and often acted more as such than as head of the church.[3]

If I rule out violent anarchism, there remains pacifist, antinationalist, anticapitalist, moral, and antidemocratic anarchism (i.e., that which is hostile to the falsified democracy of bourgeois states). There remains the anarchism which acts by means of persuasion, by the creation of small groups and networks, denouncing falsehood and oppression, aiming at

1. I prefer this title to "Old Testament" so as to avoid the charge that Christians have annexed these books and deprived the Jewish people of what really belongs to them.

2. Cf. my *Violence: Reflections from a Christian Perspective* (New York: Seabury, 1969).

3. We see the perversity of power from the fact that the pope was given a vast domain in order to free him from the political pressure exerted by kings, emperors, barons, etc., i.e., to ensure his independence, but the exact opposite was the result.

a true overturning of authorities of all kinds as people at the bottom speak and organize themselves. All this is very close to Bakunin.

But there is still the delicate point of participation in elections. Should anarchists vote? If so, should they form a party? For my part, like many anarchists, I think not. To vote is to take part in the organization of the false democracy that has been set up forcefully by the middle class. No matter whether one votes for the left or the right, the situation is the same. Again, to organize a party is necessarily to adopt a hierarchical structure and to wish to have a share in the exercise of power. We must never forget to what degree the holding of political power corrupts. When the older socialists and unionists achieved power in France in 1900-1910, one might argue that they became the worst enemies of union-ism. We have only to recall Clémenceau and Briand. This is why, in a movement that is very close to anarchy, that of ecologists, I am always opposed to political participation. I am totally hostile to the Greens movement, and in France we have seen very well what are the results of the political par-ticipation of the Ecolos (environmentalists) in elections. The movement has been split into several rival groups, three leaders have declared their hostility publicly, debates about false issues (e.g., of tactics) have clouded the true aims, money has been spent on electoral campaigns, and nothing has been gained. Indeed, the participation in elections has greatly reduced the influence of the movement. The political game can produce no important changes in our society and we must radically refuse to take part in it. Society is far too complex. Interests and structures are far too closely inte-grated into one another. We cannot hope to modify them by the political path. The example of multinationals is enough to show this. In view of global economic solidarity the left cannot change the economy of a country when it is in power.

[14]

Those who say that a global revolution is needed if we are not simply to change the government are right.

But does that mean that we are not to act at all? This is what we constantly hear when we advance a radical thesis. As if the only mode of action were political! I believe that anarchy first implies conscientious objection — to everything that constitutes our capitalist (or degenerate socialist) and imperialistic society (whether it be bourgeois, communist, white, yellow, or black). Conscientious objection is objection not merely to military service but to all the demands and obligations imposed by our society: to taxes, to vaccination, to compulsory schooling, etc.

Naturally, I am in favor of education, but only if it is adapted to children and not obligatory when children are obviously not equipped to learn intellectual data. We ought to shape education according to the children's gifts.

As regards vaccination, I have in mind a remarkable instance. A friend of mine, a doctor of law, a licentiate in mathematics, and an anarchist (or very nearly so), decided on a real return to the land. In the harsh country of the Haut-Loire he bred cattle for ten years on the high plateau. But he objected — and this is the point of the story — to the compulsory vaccination of his cattle against hoof-and-mouth disease, reckoning that if he raised them carefully, and at a distance from any other herd, there was no danger of contracting the disease. This was when matters became interesting. Veterinary officers went after him and imposed a fine. He took the case to court, giving proof of the incompetence and accidents connected with vaccination. He lost at first, but on appeal, with the help of reports from biologists and eminent veterinarians, he was triumphantly acquitted. This is a very good example of the way in which we can find a little free space in the tangle of regulations. But we have to want to do it, not dispersing our energies but attacking at a single point and winning by repulsing the administration and its rules.

We had a similar experience in our fight against the Aquitaine Coastal Commission. By enormous efforts we were able to block certain projects which would have been disastrous for the local people, but only after many court cases even at the highest levels.[4] Naturally, these are very small actions, but if we take on enough of them and are vigilant, we can check the omnipresence of the state, even though the "decentralization" noisily promoted by Defferre has made the defense of freedom much harder. For the enemy today is not the central state[5] but the omnipotence and omnipresence of administration. It is essential that we lodge objections to everything, and especially to the police and the deregulation of the judicial process. We must unmask the ideological falsehoods of the many powers, and especially we must show that the famous theory of the rule of law which lulls the democracies is a lie from beginning to end. The state does not respect its own rules. We must distrust all its offerings. We must always remember that when it pays, it calls the tune.

I recall the prevention clubs we founded in 1956 to deal with the maladjustment of young people. Our premise was

---

4. An interesting point here is that we forced the administration itself to act illegally. The method was simple. The administration began work outside the rules and had to justify itself by orders and decrees. Biasini, the director of the Commission, advanced the theory that once work has begun, even though irregularly and without a proper inquiry, etc., there is nothing more to be done. In other words, once the bulldozers set to work, there is no further recourse. This means a total regulation of citizens and an official authorization of illegality. Another example of the same kind is the building of the Île de Ré bridge, which an administrative tribunal rejected but which is going on as if nothing had happened.

5. Disastrous though its role is! For an illuminating study cf. J. J. Ledos, J. P. Jézequel, and P. Régnier, *Le gâchis audiovisuel* (Ed. Ouvrières, 1987).

that it was not the young people who were maladjusted but society itself.[6] So long as the clubs were financed in many different ways, including a subsidy, they went well and enjoyed great success, not adjusting young people to society but helping them to shape their own personalities and to replace destructive activities (drugs, etc.) with constructive and positive activities. But all that changed when the state took over the full financing, thinking under Mauroy, the minister, that it had itself invented the idea of prevention, and creating a National Council of Prevention, which was a disaster.

An important point which I must emphasize is that there have to be many efforts along the lines suggested. I have in mind one that is most important, namely, the objection to taxes. Naturally, if individual taxpayers decide not to pay their taxes, or not to pay the proportion that is devoted to military expenditures, this is no problem for the state. They are arrested and sentenced. In a matter of this kind, many people have to act together. If six thousand or twenty thousand taxpayers decide upon this type of action, the state is put in an awkward position, especially if the media are brought in. But to make this possible there has to be lengthy preparation: campaigns, conferences, tracts, etc.

More immediately practicable, though again requiring many participants, is the organizing of a school by parents on the margin of public education, though also of official private education. I have in mind a school which the parents themselves decide to organize, giving instruction in fields in which they are equipped and have authorization to teach. At the very least they might set up an alternative school like the Lycée de Saint-Nazaire started by the brother of Cohn Bendit. The most effective type is one that is run by true represen-

6. Cf. Y. Charrier and J. Ellul, *Jeunesse délinquante: Une Expérience en province* (Paris: Mercure de France, 1971).

tatives of the interested parties: the students, the parents, and the teachers.

Whenever such ventures are made, they need to be organized apart from the political, financial, administrative, and legal authorities and on a purely individual basis. An amusing personal example comes from the war days when we were refugees in a rural area. After two years we had gained the confidence and friendship of the villagers. A strange development then took place. The inhabitants knew that I had studied law and they came to consult me and to ask me to solve disputes. I thus came to play the part of an advocate, a justice of the peace, and a notary. Of course, these unpaid services had no validity in the eyes of the law, but they had validity for the parties concerned. When I had people sign an agreement settling a dispute or solving a problem, they all regarded the signatures as no less binding and authoritative than if they were official.

Naturally, these modest examples of marginal actions which repudiate authority should not cause us to neglect the need for an ideological diffusion of anarchist thinking. I believe that our own age is favorable from this standpoint in view of the absolute vacuum in relevant political thinking. The liberals still think they are in the 19th century. The socialists have no real type of socialism to offer. The communists are merely ridiculous and have hardly yet emerged from post-Stalinism. The unions are interested only in defending their position.[7] In this vacuum anarchist thinking has its opportunity if it will modernize itself and draw support from existing embryonic groups such as the ecologists.

I am thus very close to one of the forms of anarchism,

---

7. We should not forget that on the plea of safeguarding employment they supported the folly of the Concorde and still justify the manufacture and export of armaments.

and I believe that the anarchist fight is a good one. What separates me, then, from the true anarchist? Apart from the religious problem, which we shall take up again at length, I think that the point of division is as follows. The true anarchist thinks that an anarchist society — with no state, no organization, no hierarchy, and no authorities — is possible, livable, and practicable. But I do not. In other words, I believe that the anarchist fight, the struggle for an anarchist society, is essential, but I also think that the realizing of such a society is impossible. Both these points need explanation. I will begin with the second.

In truth the vision or hope of a society with neither authorities nor institutions rests on the twofold conviction that people are by nature good and that society alone is corrupt. At the extreme we find such statements as this: The police provoke robbery; abolish the police and robbery will stop. That society does in fact play a big part in perverting individuals seems sure enough to me. When there is excessive strictness, constraint, and repression, in one way or another people have to let off steam, often by violence and aggression. Today perversion in the West takes another form as well, namely, that of advertising, which promotes consumption (and robbery when people cannot afford things), also that of open pornography and violence in the media. The role of the media in the growth of delinquency and hatred of others is considerable. Nevertheless, society is not wholly responsible.

The drug policy in Holland offers an important illustration. Face-to-face with increasing drug traffic and drug use, the Dutch government opted in 1970 for a different policy from that found in other countries. To avoid the temptation of the forbidden fruit, drug use was legalized, and to check the sale of drugs the government opened centers where addicts could receive for nothing, and under medical supervision, the doses they needed. It was believed that this would halt the trade and all its evils (the bondage to dealers, the exorbitant prices, and crimes of violence to get the money). It was also believed that the craving for drugs would decline. But none of this happened. Amsterdam became the drug capital, and the center of the city holds a horrible concentration of addicts. Ending repression does not check human cravings. In spite of beliefs to the contrary, it is not a good thing.

My statement to this effect has no connection with the Christian idea of sin. Sin in effect exists only in relation to God. The mistake of centuries of Christianity has been to regard sin as a moral fault. Biblically this is not the case. Sin is a break with God and all that this entails. When I say that people are not good, I am not adopting a Christian or a moral standpoint. I am saying that their two great characteristics, no matter what their society or education, are covetousness and the desire for power. We find these traits always and everywhere. If, then, we give people complete freedom to choose, they will inevitably seek to dominate someone or something and they will inevitably covet what belongs to others, and a strange feature of covetousness is that it can never be assuaged or satisfied, for once one thing is acquired it directs its attention to something else. René Girard has fully shown what the implications of covetousness are. No society is possible among people who compete for power or who covet and find themselves coveting the same thing. As I see it, then, an ideal anarchist society can never be achieved.

It might be objected that people were originally good and that what we now see is the result of centuries of declension. My answer is that in this case we will have to allow for a transitional period, because tendencies which are so firmly rooted will not be eradicated in one generation. For how long, then, are we to retain the structures and the necessary authorities, hoping that they will adopt policies that are just and liberating and firm enough to direct us in the right path? Is our hope to be a withering away of the state? We already have experience of how this theory works out. Above all we have to remember that all power corrupts, and absolute power corrupts absolutely. This has been the experience of all millenarians and "cities of God," etc.

For my part, what seems to me to be just and possible is the creation of new institutions from the grass-roots level. The people can set up proper institutions (such as those indicated above) which will in fact replace the authorities and powers that have to be destroyed. As regards realization, then, my view is in effect close to that of the Anarcho-Syndicalists of 1880-1900. Their belief was that working-class organisms such as unions and labor halls should replace the institutions of the middle-class state. These were never to function in an authoritarian and hierarchical way but in a strictly democratic manner, and they would lead to federations, the federal bond being the only national bond.

We know, of course, what happened. At the beginning of the 1914 war the deliberate policy was to remove the better Anarcho-Syndicalists, and the union movement underwent a radical change with the appointment of permanent officials. That was the great mistake. At the same time the labor halls lost completely their original character as breeding grounds of a proletarian elite.

In sum, I have no faith in a pure anarchist society, but I do believe in the possibility of creating a new social model. The only thing is that we now have to begin afresh. The unions, the labor halls, decentralization, the federative system — all are gone. The perverse use that has been made of them has destroyed them. The matter is all the more urgent because all our political forms are exhausted and practically nonexistent. Our parliamentary and electoral system and our political parties are just as futile as dictatorships are intolerable. Nothing is left. And this nothing is increasingly aggressive, totalitarian, and omnipresent. Our experience today is the strange one of empty political institutions in which no one has any confidence any more, of a system of government which functions only in the interests of a political class, and at the same time of the almost infinite growth of power, authority, and social control which makes any one of our democracies a more authoritarian mechanism than the Napoleonic state.

This is the result of techniques. We cannot speak of a technocracy, for technicians are not formally in charge. Nevertheless, all the power of government derives from techniques, and behind the scenes technicians provide the inspiration and make things possible. There is no point here in discussing what everybody knows, namely, the growth of the state, of bureaucracy, of propaganda (disguised under the name of publicity or information), of conformity, of an express policy of making us all producers and consumers, etc. To this development there is strictly no reply. No one even puts questions.[8] The churches have once again betrayed their mission. The parties play outdated games. It is in these circumstances that I regard anarchy as the only serious challenge, as the only means of achieving awareness, as the first active step.

When I talk of a serious challenge, the point is that in anarchy there is no possibility of a rerouting into a reinforcement of power. This took place in Marxism. The very idea of a dictatorship of the proletariat presupposed power over the rest of society. Nor is it simply a matter of the power of the majority over the minority instead of the reverse. The real

8. Except for a few scientists who see the dangers of science, and a few isolated figures like C. Castoriadis.

question is that of the power of some people over others. Unfortunately, as I have said, I do not think that we can truly prevent this. But we can struggle against it. We can organize on the fringe. We can denounce not merely the abuses of power but power itself. But only anarchy says this and wants it.

In my view, then, it is more necessary than ever to promote and extend the anarchist movement. Contrary to what is thought, it can gain a broader hearing than before. Most people, living heedlessly, tanning themselves, engaging in terrorism, or becoming TV slaves, ridicule political chatter and politics. They see that there is nothing to hope for from them. They are also exasperated by bureaucratic structures and administrative bickering. If we denounce such things, we gain the ear of a large public. In a word, the more the power of the state and bureaucracy grows, the more the affirmation of anarchy is necessary as the sole and last defense of the individual, that is, of humanity. Anarchy must regain its pungency and courage. It has a bright future before it. This is why I adopt it.

2. Anarchy's Complaints against Christianity

I will try to recall here the attacks of 19th-century anarchy on Christianity and to explain myself without concealing what ought not to be. It is not a matter of justifying Christianity. I might begin by recalling the distinction I have made elsewhere between Christianity (or Christendom) and the Christian faith as we have it in the Bible.[9] I believe that the attacks on Christianity fall into two categories: the essentially historical and the metaphysical. I will begin with the former.

9. See my *Subversion of Christianity* (Grand Rapids: Eerdmans, 1986), e.g., pp. 10ff.

The first basic thesis is that religions of all kinds generate wars and conflicts which are ultimately much worse than the purely political or capricious wars of rulers, since in them the question of truth is central and the enemy, being the incarnation of evil and falsehood, has to be eliminated. This is perfectly true. It is true not only as regards traditional religions but also as regards the new religions that have replaced them: the religion of country, for example, or that of communism, or that of money. All the wars that are waged in the name of religion are inexplicable wars, as was once a Roman war. In that case the war was so atrocious that the evil it caused could not be made good by sacrifices *(piaculum)*. But our wars are inexpiable because the adversary has to be totally crushed, without exception and without pity.

The model for such wars may be found in the Bible, where at times a *herem* was declared against an enemy of the Jewish people, the point being that this hostile people had to be destroyed, women and children and even cattle being slain. Naturally, the verses that refer to the *herem* are a severe trial for believers who take the Bible seriously.

Then we have the wars waged by Islam. The principle behind these is as follows. All children born into the world are Muslims by birth. If they cease to be such, it is the fault of the parents and society. The duty of all Muslims is to bring others to the true faith. The sphere of Islam (the *umma* or community) is the whole world. No one must escape it. Hence Islam must conquer the world. The idea of the holy war *(jihad)* is the result. I do not insist on this; it is evident, and it is not my problem. Yet Islam shows more clearly than any other religion that believers are fanatics and that they are thus ready both to be killed and also to kill without restriction.

There have also been "Christian" wars. These did not begin at the first but with the Carolingian empire. The wars waged by the Christian emperors of Rome (after Constantine) were not religious. Like those of the 4th century, they were in defense of the frontiers of the empire. The idea of a religious war appeared only in the 8th century after the disintegration of the empire and the Merovingian period. My own view is that the holy wars of Christianity were in imitation of what Islam had been doing already for a century or so. War became a means to win new territories for Christianity and to force pagan peoples to become Christian. The climax came with Charlemagne, consecrated external bishop, whose action against the Saxons is well known. Having conquered part of Saxony, he gave the Saxons the choice of becoming Christians or of being put to death, and six thousand Saxons, it is said, were massacred. There then followed the long series of the Crusades, the internal wars (against the Albigenses, Cathari, etc.), and then in the 16th and 17th centuries the wars of religion in the strict sense between Protestants and Roman Catholics, with all the familiar atrocities (e.g., on the part of Cromwell). Finally, there came the "colonial" wars in which, in truth, religion was no more than a pretext or ideological cloak or justification, so that these were not really religious wars, though religion was closely implicated.

Religion, then, is incontestably a source of war. My personal response is as follows. There is a great difference between a religion that makes war a sacred duty or a ritual test (as among some Indian and African tribes) and a religion which reproves, rejects, condemns, and eliminates all violence. In the first case there is agreement between the central message that is said to be the truth and the waging of war. In the second case there is contradiction between religious revelation and the waging of war. Even though the authorities, intellectuals, and public opinion that is brought to a white heat by bellicose preaching may support the legitimacy

[25]

of a war, the duty of believers in face of it is to recall the heart of the spiritual message and to point out the radical contradiction and falsity of the call to war. Naturally, this is very difficult. Believers have to be capable of extricating themselves from the sociological current and to have the courage to oppose intellectuals and the mob. This is the problem for Christianity. I have never understood how the religion whose heart is that God is love and that we are to love our neighbors as ourselves can give rise to wars that are absolutely unjustifiable and unacceptable relative to the revelation of Jesus. I am familiar with various justifications, which we shall consider later. The immediate reality, however, is that the revelation of Jesus ought not to give rise to a religion. All religion leads to war, but the Word of God is not a religion, and it is the most serious of all betrayals to have made of it a religion.[10]

As regards the Christian faith, two questions remain, both of which link up with what follows. The first is that of truth, the second that of salvation. We have seen that one of the charges against religion is that it claims exclusive truth. This is accurate, and Christianity does not escape the charge. But what do we mean when we talk about Christian truth? The central text is the saying of Jesus: "I am the truth." Contrary to what might have been said and done later, the truth is not a collection of dogmas or conciliar or papal decisions. It is not doctrine. It is not even the Bible considered as a book. The truth is a person. It is not a question, then, of adhering to Christian doctrine. It is a question of trusting in a person who speaks to us. Christian truth can be grasped, heard, and received only in and by faith. But faith cannot be forced. The Bible tells us that. So does common sense. We cannot force someone to trust a person when there

10. See ibid., e.g., pp. 17ff.

is distrust. In no way, then, can Christian truth be imposed by violence, war, etc. Paul anticipated what might happen when he admonished us to practice the truth in love. We are to practice it, not to adopt a system of thought. This means that we are to follow Jesus, or to imitate him. But this truth is still exclusive. Hence we are to hold this truth in love. That is very hard. In church history, then, there has been constant vacillation between holding the truth without love (compulsion, etc.) and stressing love but completely neglecting the simple Gospels.

The second problem is that of salvation. A fixed idea in Christianity is that all are lost (or damned, though this is not a biblical term) unless they believe in Jesus Christ. To save them — and this is where it becomes a serious matter — we must first declare to them salvation in Jesus Christ. Yes, but suppose they will not believe in him? Progressively the idea arose that we must then force them to believe (as in the case of Charlemagne or conquests like that of Peru, etc.). The force used might be severe even to the point of threatening and carrying out a capital sentence. The great justification (as in the case of the Grand Inquisitor) is that their souls should be saved. Compared to eternal felicity, what does bodily execution matter? This execution could even be called an act of faith *(auto de fe)*. Obviously, we have here a complete reversal of the preaching of Jesus, the epistles of Paul, and also the prophets. Faith has to come to birth as a free act, not a forced one. Otherwise it has no meaning. How can we think that the God whom Jesus calls Father wants a faith under constraint? As regards all these criticisms of Christianity and Christendom, it is clear that Christians who try to be faithful to the Bible will agree that anarchists are quite right to denounce such actions and practices (i.e., the policy of violence, force, and war).

The second historical criticism is close to the first. It is that of collusion with the state. From the days of Constantine (and for many years serious historians have doubted the sincerity of his conversion, viewing it as a purely political act) the state has supposedly been Christian.[11] The church has received great help in return. Thus the state has aided it in forcing people to become "Christians." It has given it important subsidies. It has safeguarded its cultic sites. It has granted privileges to the clergy. But the church has also had to let emperors meddle in its theology, decide at times what must be its true doctrine, summon councils, supervise the appointment of bishops, etc. The church has also had to support the state. The alliance of throne and altar does not date from the Reformation but from the 5th century. Attempts were made to separate the two powers, the temporal and the spiritual, but they were constantly confused. As I noted above, the pope became the internal bishop, the emperor the external. The many ceremonies (e.g., coronations, Te Deums) had at their heart the idea that the church ought to serve the state, the political power, and guarantee the people's allegiance to it. In his cynical way Napoleon said that the clergy control the people, the bishops the clergy, and he himself the bishops. No one could state more clearly the real situation that the church was an agent of state propaganda. Obedience to the authorities was also a Christian duty. The king was divinely appointed (though dissent arose about how to state this), and therefore to disobey the king was to disobey God. But we must not generalize. I am noting here what was the official teaching, that of the higher clergy and church policy (among the Orthodox and Lutherans as well). At the base, however, among the lower clergy, the position

11. I have shown elsewhere that it is impossible for the state or society or an institution to be Christian. Since being Christian presupposes an act of faith, it is plainly impossible for an abstraction like the state.

was much less certain. As regards the period that I know best,[12] the 14th and 15th centuries, in most of the peasant revolts the clergy marched with their parishioners as revolutionaries and often headed the uprisings. But the usual outcome was a massacre.

We have to ask whether things became any different under democratic systems. Much less than one might think! The central thought is still that power is from God. Hence the democratic state is also from God. The odd thing is that this was an old idea. From the 9th century some theologians had stated that all power is from God *through the people.* Plainly, however, this did not lead directly to democracy. In "Christian" democracies we find a similar alliance to that already described, except that the church now has fewer advantages. In lay democracies there is theoretically a complete separation, but that is not in fact the case. The church has shown much theological uncertainty in this area. In France it was royalist under the kings and then became imperialist under Napoleon and republican under the Republic (with some hesitation on the part of Roman Catholics but not on that of Protestants). The prize example is that elsewhere it could even become Marxist in communist lands. Yes indeed, in Hungary and Czechoslovakia the Reformed Churches became openly communist with Hromadka and Bereczki. And in the USSR we should never forget that during the war, in 1941, Stalin asked the Orthodox Church to lend its support (e.g., by loans), and the church was happy to do so. The Orthodox Church, then, is a prop of the regime. The Roman Catholic Church is less compliant, but we must not forget that under Hitler, if it did not directly aid the regime,

12. I was Professor of the History of Institutions and I specialized in the crises of the 14th and 15th centuries, political, religious, economic, social, etc.

it did support it even in Germany. The pope even made a concordat with Hitler. The point is that no matter what the form of government, at the higher level and in its directives the church is always on the side of the state.

In the communist sphere we also call to mind a Latin American country like Nicaragua, where communism was able to install itself thanks to the Roman Catholic Church and liberation theologians. The only clear example of opposition is the well-known one of Poland.

At the same time as the churches adapted themselves to the forms of government they also adopted the corresponding ideologies. It is of interest to stress that the church in the West preached a universal Christendom covering all Europe, and transcending national differences, at the very time when the Empire was (or pretended to be) universal. Then with the breakup of the West into nations the church became national. Joan of Arc was plainly an early nationalist Christian.[13] From the 16th century wars became national, and the church always supported its own state. This led to the *Gott mit uns* which is such an object of contempt to unbelievers and such a scandal for believers. When two nations went to war, each was sure that God was on its side in an incredible distortion of biblical thinking, as though it were the elect people of the Hebrew Bible, or as though it were fighting the allegorical battle of Revelation and the political enemy were Satan.

Finally, to these manifestations of violence on the part of Christians or the churches we must add the destruction of heresies — we come back here to the idea of exclusive truth which the church represents infallibly and absolutely

---

13. Much as I admire that extraordinary woman, Joan of Arc, I think that history would have been much simpler if France had been swallowed up in a Franco-English regime!

— and the Inquisition. At this point we must be careful to distinguish. The Inquisition in the strict sense was set up in the 13th century (1229) to fight against heresies (Cathari, Albigenses) and then in the 14th century against sorcery.[14] Contrary to what is usually said, there were not really many condemnations to death or massacres. The only important instance was that of the Cathari. I have had doctoral students examine the extant records of the Inquisition for Southwest France (Bayonne, Toulouse, Bordeaux), and at most they have found only an average of six or seven condemnations a year. The Inquisition, however, was a means of controlling opinion on the one hand and inducing collective fear on the other (because of the anonymity, the secrecy of the procedure, etc.). Its very presence was enough. It then changed completely when it became an instrument of political power. Some kingdoms took it over in the 16th century, and it became a terrible instrument in their hands. Where did this happen? In Portugal, Spain, and Venice, in which it became wholly a political weapon, used not merely to induce fear but to put to death for politico-religious reasons. Already in the case of the Cathari the aim was more political than religious. The Cathari were teaching that one should not have children, and certain kings feared that this would lead to a serious drop in population.

Notwithstanding every explanation, I repeat that anarchists are right to challenge this kind of Christianity, these practices of the church, which constitute an intolerable form of power in the name of religion. In these circumstances,

---

14. It is not generally known that at first the church's attitude to sorcery was one of skepticism. Texts from the 4th to the 10th century show that parish priests were to teach the faithful that magic and sorcery do not exist! The punishing of sorcerers and witches began in the 13th century and especially in the 14th, when their numbers increased wildly due to disasters like the Black Death.

religion and power being confused, they are right to reject religion. Furthermore, although we need not insist on the point, we must also take note of the wealth of the church and prelates on the basis of exploitation of the people, and in the 19th century the association between the church and capitalist regimes. We all know what horrible use was made of the beatitude: "Blessed are the poor," and Marx was right to denounce religion as the opiate of the people. As it was preached by the church at this period, this is precisely what Christianity was.

I will say two things in conclusion. First, the situation has become much better and clearer now that the churches no longer have power, now that there is no longer a link between them and the authorities, and now that they have fewer members. Those who were in the church out of self-interest have largely left. Second, the condemnations of Christianity and the churches by anarchists (also Marxists, freethinkers, etc.) ought to be a reason, in fact, for Christians to achieve a better understanding of the biblical and evangelical message and to modify their conduct and that of the church in the light of the criticisms and their better understanding of the Bible.

Leaving the historical and moral field, we must now consider the metaphysical attacks of anarchists on religions in general and Christianity in particular. We will find in effect four decisive objections. First, we naturally run up against the slogan: No God, no Master. Anarchists, wanting no political, economic, or intellectual master, also want no religious master, no God, of whom the masters of this world, as we have seen, have made abundant use. The nub of this problem is very simply the idea of God.

Now it is true that for centuries theology has insisted that God is the absolute Master, the Lord of lords, the Almighty, before whom we are nothing. Hence it is right enough that those who reject masters will reject God too. We must also take note of the fact that even in the 20th century Christians still call God the King of creation and still call Jesus Lord even though there are few kings and lords left in the modern world. But I for my part dispute this concept of God.

I realize that it corresponds to the existing mentality. I realize that we have here a religious image of God. I realize, finally, that many biblical passages call God King or Lord. But this admitted, I contend that the Bible in reality gives us a very different image of God. We shall examine here only one aspect of this different image, though new ones also come to light and give rise to the following questions. Though the biblical God is the Almighty, in practice he does not make use of his omnipotence in his dealings with us except in particular instances which are recorded precisely because they are abnormal (e.g., the Flood, the Tower of Babel, or Sodom and Gomorrah). God's is a self-limited omnipotence, not through caprice or fancy, but because anything else would be in contradiction with his very being. For beyond power, the dominant and conditioning fact is that the being of God is love.

It is not merely Jesus who teaches this. The whole Hebrew Bible does so, at least if we read it attentively. When God creates, it is not to amuse himself, but because, being love, he wants someone to love other than himself. Nor does he create by a terrible explosion of power but by the simple Word: "God said"—no more. God does not unleash his power but expresses himself solely by his Word. This means from the very outset that he is a communicative God. By contrast, in the religious cosmogonies of the ancient Near Eastern world, the gods (including those of Olympus) are always squabbling, creating by violence, etc. In the creation of humanity, the second story (Genesis 2) shows that the word is what characterizes humanity, too. The primary role of human beings is to be those who respond to God's love. They are created to love (this is what is meant by the image of God).

Another gripping image of God is given in the story of Elijah in the wilderness (1 Kings 19). After forty days of depressing solitude, Elijah is confronted by a series of violent phenomena: a terrible fire, a wind, an earthquake. But each time the text tells us that God was not in the fire or wind or earthquake. Finally, there was a gentle murmur (A. Chouraqui translates: "the sound of a vanishing silence"), and then Elijah prostrated himself and covered his face with his mantle, for God was in this "still small voice."

Confirmation may be found in many prophetic texts in which God talks sadly to his people, making no threats. (My people, what have I done that you should turn from me?) Even when God manifests himself in power, there is never absent the aspect of what a great theologian (Karl Barth) has called the humanity of God. Thus, in the Sinai story, the mountain is encircled by thunder and lightning and the people are afraid. But Moses climbs it all the same, and the story in Exodus 33 tells us that he talked to God face-to-face, as friend to friend. Thus, no matter what God's power may be, the first aspect of God is never that of the absolute Master, the Almighty. It is that of the God who puts himself on our human level and limits himself. Theologians who were under the influence of a monarchy (whether that of Rome or that of the 16th and 17th centuries) might have insisted on omnipotence by way of imitation, but they did so by mistake. Sometimes, of course, when we have to oppose an all-powerful state, it is good that we should tell the dictator that God is more powerful than he is, that God is indeed the King of kings (as Moses told Pharaoh). When assassins put tyrants to death, tyrants soon see whether they are God. For the most part, however, the true face of the biblical God is love. And I do not believe that anarchists would be too happy with a formula that runs: No love, no master.

A second great complaint that anarchists make against Christianity relates to one of the two well-known dilemmas, namely, that if God foresees all things, if he is "providence," this rules out all human freedom. Here again we have in fact a view of God which derives from Greek philosophy and which classical theologians have greatly propagated. On the basis of Greek thought, as we all know, the Christian God was endowed with many attributes: omniscience, foreknowledge, impassibility, immutability, eternity, etc. I do not argue with what comes directly from the Bible, for example, that God is eternal, though we cannot really have any conception of what eternity is. I do claim, however, that we have made an image or representation of God which depends much more on human thought and logic than on an understanding of the Bible. The decisive contention of the Bible is always that we cannot know God, that we cannot make an image of him, that we cannot analyze what he is. The only serious theologians are those who have practiced what is called negative theology — not knowing what God is but saying only what he is not, for example, that money is not God, nor a tree, nor a spring, nor the sun. We cannot say anything positive about God. (I said above that God is love, and that is the one positive biblical declaration, but love is not a conferred "being.") This is the point of the great statement of God to Moses in Exodus 3:14: "I am who I am." The Hebrew terms can have different senses, so that various renderings of the statement are possible: "I am he who I am," "I am he who can say: I am" (as other texts put it), "I will be who I am," "I am who I will be," or "I will be who I will be." As Karl Barth said, when God reveals himself to us, he reveals himself as the Unknowable. Hence the qualities that we attribute to God come from human reason and imagination. Perhaps it is the great merit of the Death-of-God theologies not to have killed off God but to have destroyed the images that we have made of God. Undoubtedly, the attacks of the great 19th-century anarchists, as well as those of Nietzsche, were directed against the images that obtained in their period. A Protestant theologian has said that science has taught us that we no longer need the hypothesis of God to reach an understanding of phenomena. Ricoeur, a Christian philosopher, has often raised the question of the God of the gaps (i.e., appealing to God when we do not understand something). The mistake is to make of God either an explanatory God of the gaps or a useful hypothesis to explain the origin of the universe. But we are now returning to the simple and essentially biblical truth that God does not serve any outside purpose.[15]

But, one might say, why then preserve this God? Why not preserve only that which is useful, which serves some purpose? To say this is to give evidence of a utilitarianism and modernism in the very worst taste! It was a serious mistake to try to make God useful along these lines. But if God is not of this kind, we need to challenge a common notion, namely, that of providence. The idea of a power which foresees and ordains and controls all things is a curious one that has nothing Christian about it. There is no providence in the Bible, no God who distributes blessings, sicknesses, wealth, or happiness. Is God a giant computer functioning according to a program? There is nothing biblical about an idea of that kind. In the Bible there is a God who is with us, who accompanies us in our ventures. This God can at times intervene but not according

15. Readers will undoubtedly argue that the first chapters of Genesis explain how things began. They do not. The point of these chapters is very different. The rabbis had no interest in origins.

[36]

Anarchy from a Christian Standpoint

to set laws or dictatorial caprice. There is no God of providence. We shall have to see why later on. If I believe, I may
regard this blessing as a gift of God and this misfortune as a
warning or punishment from God. The essential thing, however, is to understand that there is no objective knowledge of
God. I cannot objectively proclaim (especially in the case of
others) that one thing is a divine gift and another a divine
chastisement. This is a matter of faith and it is thus subjective.
Hence when someone says something to me, I may in faith
hear more than the actual words state, perhaps finding in them
a Word of God. Is all that an illusion? But why should what is
subjective be an illusion? Experience over hundreds of years
proves the contrary.

Let us continue, however, to hunt down the mistaken
images of God that Christians have fabricated. If providence
is a popular one, intellectuals have invented a God who is
the first cause (on the basis of scientific causalism). Naturally,
this can be maintained metaphysically, but never biblically.
The basic reason for this is that the God who is a first cause
belongs to an essentially mechanical system, but the God
whom the Bible portrays is changing and fluid. He makes
decisions that might seem to be arbitrary. He is a free God.
As Kierkegaard says, he is supremely the Unconditioned. He
cannot sit on top of a pyramid of causes. This brings us to
an even more basic point.

Genesis 1 describes a six-day creation. (Naturally, we are
not to think of twenty-four-hour days.) Creation is complete
on the sixth day. God saw that everything was very good. Then
on the seventh day he rested. But where does all human history
fit in? The only possible answer is that it takes place on the
seventh day.[16] God enters into his rest and the human race

16. For a full explanation cf. my *What I Believe* (Grand Rapids: Eerdmans, 1989), pp. 152-66.

[37]

begins its history. It has a specific place in creation. Creation has its own laws of organization and functioning. The race has a part to play in it. It has a certain responsibility. The fact that it proceeds to disobey God, that is, to break with him, does not alter the situation in any way. God does not begin again. He does not leave his rest in order to direct operations. The organization of the world remains the same. But we must not forget what we said above. God continues to love this creature and he waits to be loved by this creature. He is Word, and he wills to continue dialogue with this creature. Furthermore, at times he leaves his rest. Many biblical texts say this expressly. And at the end, in Hebrews and Revelation, the great promise and joy is that of refinding rest. God will find his rest again and we shall enter into this rest of God (which has nothing whatever to do with the rest of death).

At times God comes out of his rest. When the human situation becomes desperate, God devises a plan of rescue. This may not always succeed, for we humans have to take part in it, and we may fail. There are many examples. Again, God comes out of his rest because human wickedness in relation to others becomes so intolerable that he has to intervene (though not, as I have said, with stupefying wonders) and provisionally to reestablish an order in which the wicked are punished (although by others, to whom God secretly gives his power). What is hardest to understand if we are used to traditional concepts of God is the intermingling of human history with God's history.

This brings us to a central notion. Far from being the universal Commander, the biblical God is above all the Liberator.[17] What is not generally known is that Genesis is not

17. Cf. my *Ethique de la liberté,* 3 vols. (Geneva: Labor et Fides, 1975-1984) (condensed Eng. trans. *Ethics of Freedom* [Grand Rapids: Eerdmans, 1976]).

really the first book of the Bible. The Jews regard Exodus as
the basic book. They primarily see in God not the universal
Creator but their Liberator. The statement is impressive: "I
have liberated you from Egypt, the house of bondage" (cf.
Exodus 13:14; 20:2). In Hebrew, Egypt is called *Mitsraim,*
and the meaning of this term is "twofold anguish," which
the rabbis explain as the anguish of living and the anguish
of dying. The biblical God is above all the one who liberates
us from all bondage, from the anguish of living and the
anguish of dying. Each time that he intervenes it is to give
us again the air of freedom. The cost is high. And it is through
human beings that God discharges this mission, mostly
human beings who at first are frightened and refuse, as we
see from the many examples of God's pedagogy, by which
Alphonse Maillot shows how full of humor the biblical God
is.

But why freedom? If we accept that God is love, and
that it is human beings who are to respond to this love, the
explanation is simple. Love cannot be forced, ordered, or
made obligatory. It is necessarily free. If God liberates, it is
because he expects and hopes that we will come to know him
and love him. He cannot lead us to do so by terrorizing us.

I realize that one might lodge objections. This God is
also the one who gave the Jewish people hundreds of commandments, primarily the Decalogue. How can we say, then,
that he does not force us? I am again amazed that we can
treat these commandments as though they were the equivalent of the articles in a human code, deriving from them
obligations and duties. We have to view them very differently.
First, these commandments are the border that God draws
between life and death. If you do not kill, you have the best
chance of not being killed. But if you commit a murder, it is
almost certain that you will die in consequence. (Nor is there
any difference between private crime and war!) Those who

take to the sword will be killed by the sword. This is true of all the commandments. If you stay within them, your life is protected. If you break them, you enter a world of risks and dangers. "See, I set before you good and life, evil and death. Therefore choose good [I, God, counsel and implore you to do so], so that you may live" (cf. Deuteronomy 30:19). Second, these commandments are more a promise than an order. You shall not kill also means that you will not have to kill. God promises that it will be possible not to kill.

God's liberating action for us, so far as the Christian faith is concerned, comes to fulfilment in Jesus Christ. The one who insists the most on this freedom is Paul. Liberty is the theme of his Epistles to the Corinthians. It is for freedom that we are freed. We have been freed and must not become the slaves of anything. All things are lawful but not all are expedient. James, too, calls the law of God the law of liberty. Amazingly, Paul finds no place for precepts on food or life-style. Such precepts, he says, have an appearance of wisdom but they are merely human commandments and not the commandments of God. When we read such passages, we find it hard to understand how the churches have derived the very opposite from them, heaping up moral precepts and treating their members as subjects and even as infants.

We are thus liberated. We have to take up our responsibilities. Nevertheless, God acts. There are divine interventions and divine orders. How are we to understand this? My first point is that God's commandments are always addressed to individuals. God chooses this or that person to do something specific. It is not a matter of a general law. We have no right to generalize the order. At most we may draw a lesson from it. Thus Jesus tells the rich young ruler to sell all his goods, to give to the poor, and to follow him. We must not generalize this command. We must not decide that all Christians have to sell their goods, etc. But the saying is designed to put us all on guard against riches. Individual Christians, if conscience so dictates, may also take the command as specifically addressed to them. The main point in this context, however, is to see that we are confronted here by a divine-human dialectic. We ourselves are free to act and are responsible for our acts. But God also acts in each situation. The two actions then combine or oppose one another. In any case, we are never passive. God does not do everything. He can give counsel or issue an order, but he does not prevent us from taking a different course. Eventually — an astonishing situation — he might approve of us even though we do not do as he wills. (We recall the extraordinary wish of Job that God would find himself in the wrong and Job in the right.) In other words, the biblical God is not a machine, a big computer, with which we cannot reason and which functions according to a program. Nor are we robots for God who have to execute the decisions of him who made us.

This leads us to what is (to the best of my knowledge) the last and great objection of anarchists against God. It consists of the famous dilemma: Either God is omnipotent but in view of the evil on earth he is not good (since it is he who does all that takes place), or God is good but he is not omnipotent, since he cannot prevent the evil that is done. I believe that what we have already said will facilitate our reply. First, we must make it clear that evil is not the product of some higher force, that is, Satan, the devil, etc. What we have here are not realities but mythical representations. The terms are general ones in Hebrew and Greek, not proper names. Mephistopheles is a legendary figure, not a biblical one. All that which causes division between people (the very opposite of love) is the devil. Satan is the accuser, that is, that which causes people to bring accusations against one another. Evil derives from us in the twofold sense that we wrong ourselves and others and harm our neighbors, nature, etc. There is no dualism of a good God and a bad god. What we have are not evil beings but evil forces. The evil one stands for false intellectual questions. The great serpent is the force that drives the world to destruction. But biblically it is we ourselves who are the issue, and we alone.

As we have seen, God calls us to turn to himself in love. Constantly, then, he intervenes to liberate us. Being free, we can ourselves decide. We can wrong and injure. We can do the opposite of what God wills. God wills the good, but he leaves us free to do the opposite. If he did not, if as the Almighty he made us automatically do the good, human life would no longer have any meaning. We would be robots in his hand, toys that he has made (but why?). Note well that if this were so, we would no longer be responsible for anything and it would be of no importance whether we did good or evil. "Things" would no doubt function impeccably. There would be no more wars, murders, dictatorships, etc. There would be no more computers! What about natural accidents? Cataclysms? This is obviously the point of greatest difficulty for agnostics. The biblical explanation is that since creation is made as a whole, all its parts are in strictest solidarity with one another (as the most advanced physicists now admit), and since in this creation human beings are the crown of the work and are also responsible for creation, their role being to carry God's love to it, all creation is implicated in their break with God. Now that the principal part of creation has decided to seize its autonomy and go its own way, nothing within creation is left intact. The result is bad. Nevertheless, the laws of the organization of the cosmos and matter remain, just as the human body is preserved. There is no return to chaos. Like human life, however, the universe is now subject to rents and accidents. This is inevitable, since humanity has broken with him who is being itself.

A final point, however, is that what we call cataclysms

are so only for us and relative to us. An avalanche, earthquake, or flood is not bad in itself. It does not cause any particular damage to nature. Often it is simply an expression of physical or chemical laws that we have set in motion. It is terrible only because we are there and suffer the consequences of natural changes that we call cataclysms relative to us. As we have said, God does not intervene incessantly. He does not stop the functioning of natural laws because we are there, we who have broken with him! He does so only in the exceptional cases that Christians call miracles. And we need to insist again and again that the material fact of a miracle is not at all the important thing from the biblical standpoint. The important thing is simply the meaning that we find in it, and especially the sign it gives that relationship with God is reestablished, as God shows by protecting, healing, etc. A miracle is not a marvel. It is also very rare and exceptional. I thus reject totally, for example, the miracle attributed to the child Jesus (making birds out of clay and breathing upon them to make them fly). Miracles of this sort which some later texts record have no other aim than that of dumbfounding those who see them. Jesus himself, however, never performed miracles in order to astonish people or to make them see in him the Son of God. He expressly refused to do this. Finally, I also reject totally the well-known apparitions (of the Virgin or of angels) which have nothing whatever to do with what the Bible teaches us about God's action.

Having said all this, I make no pretense at all of having convinced my readers. My only effort has been to put the questions better so that those who claim to be atheists or agnostics may do so for good reasons and not for reasons that are false or fanciful. When I used to teach an annual course on Marx and Marxism (1947-1979), I always told my students that I was trying to be as honest as possible, that I was not seeking to convince them either one way or the other, that what I wanted was that when they decided either to be for Marxism or against it they should not do so out of emotion or with vague ideas or because of a certain background, but with a precise knowledge and for good reasons. I would say the same here and now.

II. *The Bible as the Source of Anarchy*

My next task is to show by a "naive" reading of the Bible that far from offering us a sure basis for the state and the authorities, a better understanding will, I believe, point us toward anarchy; not, of course, in the common sense of disorder, but in the sense of *an-arche:* no authority, no domination. We commonly talk of sheer anarchy when we see disorder. This is because we in the West are convinced that order can be established in society only by a strong central power and by force (police, army, propaganda). To challenge power of this kind necessarily means disorder! Luther, for instance, was so frightened by the disorder of the Peasants' Revolt (a consequence of his preaching of Christian liberty, which peasant groups accepted and wanted to manifest at once) that he quickly called upon the princes to suppress the uprisings. Calvin could even say that anything is better than social disorder, even tyranny! I quote these two authors because they are the closest to me (as a Protestant) and in order to show that even faithful readers of the Bible and true Christians can be blinded by the obvious usefulness of kings, princes, etc. They can read the Bible only through this filter.

But today, confronted with the crushing of individuals by the state under every regime, we need to challenge this Behemoth and therefore to read the Bible differently. It is true enough, as we shall see, that there are also in the Bible texts which seem to validate authority. But as I will show, I believe that there is a general current which points toward anarchy, the passages that favor authority being exceptions.

1. The Hebrew Bible

After its liberation from Egypt, the Hebrew people was first led by a charismatic head, and during its forty years of desert wandering it really had no precise organization (in spite of certain hints in Exodus). To invade and conquer Canaan it then had a military leader, Joshua, but this was only for a short time. (Some scholars doubt indeed whether the Hebrew people was a single group of identical origin.) As already sketched out, perhaps by Moses, the people settled by clans and tribes. The twelve tribes all had their own heads, but these had little concrete authority. When an important decision had to be made, with ritual sacrifices and prayers for divine inspiration, a popular assembly was held and this had the last word. After Joshua each tribe set about occupying its own territory, for many of the areas, although assigned, had not yet been fully conquered! When the tribes had completed the occupation, an interesting system was organized. There were no tribal princes. Families that might be regarded as aristocratic were either destroyed or vanquished. The God of Israel declared that he and he alone would be Israel's head. Yet this was not a theocracy, for God had no representative on earth and tribal assemblies made the decisions.

An exception was when the situation became disastrous

through successive defeats, through famine, through social disorder, or through idolatry and a return to pagan religions. God then chose a man or a woman who had no specific authority but whom he inspired to win a war or to lead the people back to reverence for God, that is, to resolve the crisis. Apparently when the "judges"[1] had played their part they effaced themselves and rejoined the people. This was obviously a flexible system. God did not necessarily choose people of distinguished family or health. Deborah, Gideon, Tola, Jair, and Samson were more prophets than kings. They had no permanent power. God alone could be considered the supreme authority. A significant phrase at the end of the book of Judges (21:25) is that at that time there was no king in Israel; people did what was right in their own eyes. Proof may be found in the story of Abimelech in ch. 9.

One of the sons of Gideon, with no mandate from God, decided that since he was of the family of him who had saved Israel, he ought to succeed his father in office. He began by assassinating all his brothers. He then assembled the inhabitants of Shechem and Millo (or Beth-millo) and proclaimed himself king. But the prophet Jotham opposed him, and addressing the people he told them an interesting parable. The trees gathered to elect a king and put him at their head. They chose the olive. But the olive refused, saying that its job was to produce good oil. They then chose the fig, but it made a similar response: "Shall I give up my sweetness and the excellent fruit which I bear in order to be above the other trees?" (v. 9). But the trees wanted a king. They chose the vine, but the vine answered like the first two. They then approached the bramble, which accepted and stated at once that those which disobeyed it would be burned by it. Having

1. These were not judges in our sense but leaders of the people who also showed them where justice resides and what it is.

[47]

denounced Abimelech, Jotham had to flee. Abimelech reigned for three years. The Israelites, accustomed to freedom, then began to revolt. Oppression and massacres resulted. But after his victories over the rebels, Abimelech was passing a tower and a woman up in the tower threw a piece of millstone on his head and crushed his skull. The system of judges was then restored.

The real history of royal power (i.e., central and unified power) would begin only with the familiar story in 1 Samuel (ch. 8). Samuel was now judge. But the assembled people told him that they had now had enough of this political system. They wanted a king so as to be like other nations.[2] They also thought that a king would be a better military leader. Samuel protested and went to God in prayer. The God of Israel replied: Do not be upset. The people have not rejected you, Samuel, but me, God. They have constantly rejected me since I liberated them. Accept their demand but warn them of what will happen.[3] Hence Samuel returned to the assembly of the people of Israel and told them that since they wanted a king, they should have one. But they had to know what this king would do. He would take their sons and make soldiers of them. He would take their daughters for his harem or as domestic servants. He would impose taxes and confiscate the best lands. . . . The people replied, however, that they did not care. They wanted a king. Samuel warned them again that they would cry out against this king. But nothing could be done. He who was chosen to be king thus came on the scene, namely, Saul, who, as we know, became

2. We note here the attraction of the centralized state. The same thing has been seen in Africa since 1950, as the African peoples have wanted states after the Western model.

3. We need to see that this is exactly what the prophets would do, not predicting the future but warning people of what would happen if they persisted in their chosen path.

mad, committed all kinds of abuses of power, and was finally killed in battle against the Philistines.

The second king, David, enjoyed great renown. He was Israel's greatest monarch. He was constantly held up as a model. I have written elsewhere that he was the exception among Israel's kings. But Vernard Eller is harsher than I am.[4] He thinks that David is a good example in favor of anarchy. A first reason is that one of the passages (2 Samuel 12:7-9) shows us that David did nothing on his own. It was God alone who acted through him. His glory owed nothing to his *arche* but solely to God's benevolence. Eller then shows that during his reign David did all the things that in later centuries would bring successive disasters on Israel's kings. This is obviously important. (In France Louis XIV would do all the things which led to the political mistakes of the 18th century and hence to the revolution.) Furthermore, the Bible curiously insists upon all David's faults: the killing of his rivals, arranging the death of the husband of a woman whom he desired, the incessant civil wars of his reign, etc., so that David is not presented as in any way blameless or glorious.

After David came Solomon his son. Solomon was just and upright. But then power went to his head, as it did with others. He imposed crushing taxes, built ruinous palaces, and took 700 wives and 300 concubines! He began to worship other gods besides the God of Israel. He built fortresses over the whole land. When he died he was hated by everyone.

The elders of Israel advised Solomon's son and designated successor to adopt a more liberal policy, reducing taxes and the heavy yoke of servitude. But Rehoboam did not listen to them, and when the people reassembled he told them: "My father made your yoke heavy, but I will make it still

---

4. See Eller, *Christian Anarchy* (Grand Rapids: Eerdmans, 1987), pp. 8-9.

heavier; my father chastised you with whips, but I will chastise you with scorpions" (1 Kings 12:14). The people revolted. They stoned his finance minister. They rejected the house of David. A division took place. The tribe of Judah stayed loyal to Rehoboam. The other tribes rallied around a former minister of Solomon, Jeroboam.

In my view this whole story is worth telling because it shows how severe the Bible is even on the "great" kings. It is severe precisely to the degree that these kings represented in their day the equivalent of a state: an army, a treasury, an administration, centralization, etc.

Yet this does not exhaust what we have to say about Israel's monarchy. Two important points have still to be made. The first can be summarized briefly. We can say that in the biblical accounts "good" kings are always defeated by Israel's enemies, and the "great" kings who win victories and extend their borders are always "bad." "Good" means that they are just, that they do not abuse their power, and that they worship the true God of Israel. "Bad" means that they promote idolatry, reject God, and are also unjust and wicked. The presentation is so systematic that some modern historians suggest that the accounts were written by antimonarchists and partisans. (It is true that in Chronicles the presentation is much less clear-cut.) The astounding thing to me is that the texts were edited, published, and authorized by rabbis and representatives of the people (if one can say that) at a time when the kings in question were reigning. There must have been censorship and controls, and yet these did not prevent the writings from being circulated. Furthermore, the accounts were not merely preserved but were also regarded as divinely inspired. They were treated as a revelation of the God of Israel, who is thus presented as himself an enemy of royal power and the state. They were sacred texts. They were included in the body of inspired texts (there was as yet no canon). They were read in the synagogues (even though they must have seemed like antiroyalist propaganda to rulers like Ahab). They were commented upon as the Word of God in the presence of all the people. This is to me an astonishing fact which gives evidence of the dominant thinking of the Jewish people from the 8th to the 4th century B.C.

In addition, the same texts and all the prophetic books bring to light a politically very odd phenomenon, namely, that for every king there was a prophet. The prophet (e.g., in the case of David) was most often a severe critic of royal acts. He claimed to come from God and to carry a word from God. This Word was always in opposition to royal power. Naturally, the prophets were often expelled; they were obliged to flee; they were put in prison; they were threatened with death, etc. But this did not make any difference. Their judgment was regarded as the truth. And again their writings, usually in opposition to power, were preserved, were regarded as a revelation of God, and were listened to by the people. None of them came to the aid of a king; none was a royal counselor; none was "integrated." The prophets were a counterforce, as we might put it today. This counterforce did not represent the people — it represented God. Even idolatrous kings found it very hard to deal with these representatives of God in whom the people believed. The prophets stated unceasingly that the kings were mistaken, that the policies they were pursuing would have such and such consequences which had to be viewed as a divine judgment. Sometimes the kings appealed to others who also claimed to be speaking in God's name and to be prophets. There was thus a battle of prophets. But the accounts preserved under Isaiah and Jeremiah show that each time the true prophets prevailed against the false. Here again we find the same strange phenomenon as before. None of the false prophecies that were favorable to the kings has been preserved in the holy scriptures. The struggles of the true prophets have been preserved, however, and the fact that logically the royal authority ought to have suppressed them shows that we have in their declarations the Word of God. As I see it, these facts manifest in an astounding way the constancy of an antiroyalist if not an antistatist sentiment.

We are not yet done. We have to add two further factors. Toward the end of the 4th century B.C. we come across an astonishing book which is usually called Ecclesiastes (or Qohelet). This book seriously challenges political power.[5] It is supposedly the work of Solomon, the great king, the most wealthy and the most powerful. But from the very first Solomon learns that political power is vanity and a pursuit of wind. He has obtained all that royal power can give. He has built palaces and promoted the arts. But none of that amounts to anything. Nor is that the only criticism of political power. In 3:16 we are told that "in the place established to judge among humans, wickedness is always established, and in the place established to proclaim justice, there is wickedness." The author also sees the evil that there is in what we would now call bureaucracy (a child of hierarchy). "If you see in a province the poor oppressed and the violation of law and of justice, do not be surprised, for the person who is in charge is watched by a higher, and above them there are yet higher ones." And this text concludes ironically: "an advantage for the people is a king honored by the land" (5:8-9). But then there is a virulent attack on all domination: "A person lords it over a person to make him miserable" (8:9). Finally, irony again: "Do not curse the king, do not curse the rich in your bedchamber, for a bird of the air will carry your voice, or some winged creature will tell your

5. Cf. my *Reason for Being: A Meditation on Ecclesiastes* (Grand Rapids: Eerdmans, 1990).

words" (10:20). Thus the political power has spies everywhere, and even in your bedroom, do not say anything against it, if you want to go on living!

In conclusion we must look at the end of the Jewish monarchy. Palestine was conquered by the Greeks and then became part of the Seleucid kingdom (end of the 3rd century B.C.). Then came the Maccabean revolt to liberate Judea and especially Jerusalem. The war of liberation was long and bloody, but success came in 163 B.C. Many political parties then struggled for power. From a colonial dictatorship the Jews fell under a Jewish dictatorship, the Hasmonean monarchy, which was not only very corrupt but was characterized by palace intrigues (one king starved his mother to death, another assassinated his brothers, etc.). These things made pious Jews hostile to this dynasty, and the people were so disgusted that they preferred to appeal to a foreign king to rid them of their Israelite king. The deposition did not succeed, but we have here an explanation of the hostility to all political power that prevailed in the 1st century B.C.

The story of the collapse of Israel's monarchy was not yet at an end. The Romans came on the scene in Palestine in 65 B.C. Pompey besieged Jerusalem and finally took it, a horrible massacre following. When Pompey celebrated his triumph at Rome, Aristobulus, the last Hasmonean king, was among his prisoners. An abominable struggle for the succession then began among the leading Jewish families. Obviously, the law of God and the solidarity of faith meant nothing to the leaders.

It was Herod, the son of a protégé of Caesar, who was appointed governor of Galilee by the Romans. Herod adopted a harsh policy and restored order in what had become a world of dismal brigandage. He put the main brigand leader to death. (Guerrilla attacks on the political authorities had now become pure and simple banditry.) His enemies accused him before the supreme "political" court, the Sanhedrin (which did nothing and had no real power), on the ground that he had usurped this court's prerogative, it alone having the power of life and death. But Herod, who knew that he had Roman support, showed such assurance and arrogance before the Sanhedrin that this timid body did not dare do anything against him. Herod returned to Jerusalem with an army but his father intervened to prevent a new war. His power progressively increased. In 37 B.C. he became the true king of all Palestine in alliance with Rome. A governor ruled with him, but he was not under the governor. He depended directly on the *princeps* (later emperor) of Rome.

Equipped with such power, he engaged in considerable political activity. He imposed a tight administration on the whole country with police control. He also began construction. He built whole cities in honor of Augustus and a magnificent temple of Augustus (he was one of those who spread the emperor cult in the East). He also built strong fortifications at Jerusalem. Finally, in 20 B.C. he began building a new temple (as we see, he was eclectic) for the God of Israel. He enlarged the esplanade (with enormous supporting walls that may still be seen, one of them being the famous Wailing Wall). He also put up a sumptuous structure with ornaments of gold, etc. He thus came to be known as Herod the Great. But he could engage in this construction program only by imposing heavy taxes and oppressing the people, even to the point of forced labor. Nor should we forget that after him the country would be delivered up to 150 years of civil war and incomparable devastation. The land was ruined and there were frequent famines. Violence and terror were the instruments of government, as we can well imagine. The only reality that counted for Herod was the friendship and support of Rome and the emperor.

Herod died in A.D. 4 and the disputed succession gave

rise to new civil wars. Rome then seized one part of Herod's kingdom. Finally, one of his sons, Herod Antipas, carried the day and regained part of the kingdom. Antipas led a completely insane life of crime and debauchery. We need to note this if we are to understand what followed. How did the people of Israel react to the rule of Rome on the one side (which was less severe than that of the Jewish crown) and the violence of the Herods on the other? (The curious thing is that, except for the book of Daniel, no more writings were recognized by the people and the rabbis as divinely inspired. Up to John the Baptist there were no more prophets.) What we find are two reactions. The one was violent. This unworthy dynasty and the Roman invaders must be chased out of the country. The country, then, was not merely prey to conflicts among its leaders. It was also in ferment due to the activity of guerrilla bands (then called brigands) who fought the royal house and Rome by the usual methods: attacks, assassinations of prominent people, etc. The other reaction, that of the devout, was one of withdrawal from this horrible situation. These pious people established fervent religious communities, avoided secular matters, and devoted themselves solely to prayer and worship. Among them there developed an apocalyptic trend, on the one hand prophesying the end of the world (which had long since been announced: When you see the abomination of desolation standing where it ought not — how better describe the Hasmonean and Herodian dynasties?), and on the other hand expecting the coming of God's Messiah who would set everything in order and reestablish the kingdom of God.

In their different ways both reactions ascribed no value to the state, to political authority, or to the organization of that authority.

2. Jesus

This was the general climate into which Jesus was born. The first event that Matthew's Gospel records concerning him is not without interest. Herod the Great was still in power. He learned that a child had been born in Bethelehem and that reports were circulating that this child would be Israel's Messiah. He realized at once what trouble this might cause him and he thus ordered that all the children of two years and under in Bethlehem and vicinity should be killed. The accuracy of this account is irrelevant for my purpose. The important thing is that we have the story, that it was abroad among the people, and that the first Christians accepted it (we must not forget that they were Jews) and put it in a text which they regarded as divinely inspired. This shows what their view was of Herod, and behind him of power. This was the first contact of the infant Jesus with political power. I am not saying that it influenced his later attitude to it, but undoubtedly it left a mark upon his infancy.

What I really want to point out here by means of a series of recorded incidents is not that Jesus was an enemy of power but that he treated it with disdain and did not accord it any authority. In every form he challenged it radically. He did not use violent methods to destroy it. In recent years there has been much talk of a guerrilla Jesus who, the people thought, would chase out the Romans. I think that there are two mistakes here. Nothing supports the account of a guerrilla Jesus such as we find, for example, in P. Cardonnel, who concludes from the cleansing of the temple and the request of Jesus for two swords that the disciples had a stock of arms. A single fact shows how impossible is that theory. Among the disciples there were Zealots (Simon and Judas), who supported violence, but also collaborators with the Romans (Matthew), and the two groups were able to get on well together. Jesus never extolled violence; if he was a guerrilla head, the least we can say is that he was a fool. His travels, especially the last journey to Jerusalem, made no tactical sense, and they inevitably led to his arrest.

Another and even more widespread error is that all the Jews were essentially preoccupied with expelling the Roman invaders. Undoubtedly, there was hatred for the *goyim* and a desire to chase out the invaders. The massacres perpetrated by the Romans were constantly remembered. But that was not all. In addition, patriotic Jews could not forget that the kings of Judea had been appointed by the Romans and could not remain in power without their support. Hatred of the Romans combined with a desire to be rid of the Herods. Even among pious sects like the Essenes there was expectation of the coming of a mysterious personage who as a Teacher of Righteousness would not have political power but who would give true freedom to the Jewish people by establishing not temporal and military power but spiritual power, as we see also in certain Jewish apocalypses of the period. I would not venture to say that these sects had an anarchist hope, but many of the texts suggest it.

When Jesus began his public ministry, the Gospels tell the story of his temptation. The devil tempts him three times. The important temptation in this context is the last (in Matthew). The enemy takes Jesus to a high mountain and shows him all the kingdoms of the world and their glory: "I will give you all these things, if you will prostrate yourself and worship me" (Matthew 4:8-9), or: "I will give you all this power and the glory of these kingdoms, for it has been given to me, and I give it to whom I will. If you, then, will prostrate yourself before me, it shall all be yours" (Luke 4:6-7). Again, my concern is not with the facticity of the records nor with theological problems. My concern is with the views of the writers, with the personal convictions that they express here.

It is not unimportant to emphasize, perhaps, that the two Gospels were probably written with Christian communities of Greek origin in view, not Jews who were influenced by the hatred to which we referred above. The reference in these texts, then, is to political power in general ("all the kingdoms of the world") and not just the Herod monarchy. And the extraordinary thing is that according to these texts all powers, all the power and glory of the kingdoms, all that has to do with politics and political authority, belongs to the devil. It has all been given to him and he gives it to whom he wills. Those who hold political power receive it from him and depend upon him. (It is astonishing that in the innumerable theological discussions of the legitimacy of political power, no one has ever adduced these texts!) This fact is no less important than the fact that Jesus rejects the devil's offer. Jesus does not say to the devil: It is not true. You do not have power over kingdoms and states. He does not dispute this claim. He refuses the offer of power because the devil demands that he should fall down before him and worship him. This is the sole point when he says: "You shall worship the Lord your God and you shall serve him, only him" (Matthew 4:10). We may thus say that among Jesus' immediate followers and in the first Christian generation political authorities — what we call the state — belonged to the devil and those who held power received it from him. We have to remember this when we study the trial of Jesus.

A further question is why reference is here made to the devil. The *diabolos* is etymologically the "divider" (not a person). The state and politics are thus primary reasons for division. This is the point of the reference to the devil. We do not have here a primitive and simplistic image or an arbitrary designation. What we have is a judgment which is not in the least religious and which expresses both experience and reflection. This judgment was obviously facilitated by the horrible lacerations caused among the people by the Hasmonean and Herodian dynasties and the ensuing uprisings and civil conflict. However that may be, the first Christian generation was globally hostile to political power and regarded it as bad no matter what its orientation or constitutional structures.

We now come to texts which record Jesus' own sayings and which exegetes regard as in all probability authentic. We do not have here early Christian interpretation but the position of Jesus himself (which, evidently, was the source of this early Christian interpretation). There are five main sayings.

Naturally, the first is the famous saying: "Render to Caesar." I will briefly recall the story (Mark 12:13ff.). The enemies of Jesus were trying to entrap him, and the Herodians put the question. Having complimented Jesus on his wisdom, they asked him whether taxes should be paid to the emperor: "Is it lawful to pay the taxes to Caesar or not? Should we pay, or should we not pay?" The question itself is illuminating. As the text tells us, they were trying to use Jesus' own words to trap him. If they put this question, then, it was because it was already being debated. Jesus had the reputation of being hostile to Caesar. If they could raise this question with a view to being able to accuse Jesus to the Romans, stories must have been circulating that he was telling people not to pay taxes. As he often does, Jesus avoids the trap by making an ironical reply: "Bring me a coin, and let me look at it." When this is done, he himself puts a question: "Whose likeness and inscription is this?" It was evidently a Roman coin. One of the skillful means of integration used by the Romans was to circulate their own money throughout the empire. This became the basic coinage against which all others were measured. The Herodians replied to Jesus: "Caesar's." Now we need to realize that in the Roman world an individual mark on an object denoted ownership, like cattle brands in the American West in the 19th century.

The mark was the only way in which ownership could be recognized. In the composite structure of the Roman empire it applied to all goods. People all had their own marks, whether a seal, stamp, or painted sign. The head of Caesar on this coin was more than a decoration or a mark of honor. It signified that all the money in circulation in the empire belonged to Caesar. This was very important. Those who held the coins were very precarious owners. They never really owned the bronze or silver pieces. Whenever an emperor died, the likeness was changed. Caesar was the sole proprietor. Jesus, then, had a very simple answer: "Render to Caesar that which is Caesar's." You find his likeness on the coin. The coin, then, belongs to him. Give it back to him when he demands it.

With this answer Jesus does not say that taxes are lawful. He does not counsel obedience to the Romans. He simply faces up to the evidence. But what really belongs to Caesar? The excellent example used by Jesus makes this plain: Whatever bears his mark! Here is the basis and limit of his power. But where is this mark? On coins, on public monuments, and on certain altars. That is all. Render to Caesar. You can pay the tax. Doing so is without importance or significance, for all money belongs to Caesar, and if he wanted he could simply confiscate it. Paying or not paying taxes is not a basic question; it is not even a true political question.

On the other hand, whatever does not bear Caesar's mark does not belong to him. It all belongs to God.[6] This is where the real conscientious objection arises. Caesar has no right whatever to the rest. First we have life. Caesar has no

6. It is extraordinary that J.-J. Rousseau attacked this saying (*Social Contract*, IV, 8) on the ground that setting the kingdom of Caesar and the kingdom of God in antithesis generates internal divisions which break up nations. All institutions that bring humanity into self-contradiction, says Rousseau, must be rejected. His conclusion, then, is that the state must be the great master of a "civil religion," i.e., a state religion!

[60]

right of life and death. Caesar has no right to plunge people into war. Caesar has no right to devastate and ruin a country. Caesar's domain is very limited. We may oppose most of his pretensions in the name of God. Jesus challenges the Herodians, then, for they can have no objections to what he says. They, too, were Jews, and since the text tells us that those who put the question were Pharisees as well as Herodians, we can be certain that some of them were devout Jews. Hence they could not contest the statement of Jesus that all the rest is God's. At the same time Jesus was replying indirectly to the Zealots who wanted to transform the struggle for the liberation of Israel into a political struggle. He reminded them what was the limit as well as the basis of the struggle.

The second saying of Jesus about political authorities comes in an astonishing discussion. The disciples were accompanying him to Jerusalem, where some of them seem to have thought that he would seize power. They were arguing who would be closest to him when he entered upon his kingly rule (Matthew 20:20-25). The wife of Zebedee presented her two sons, James and John, and made the express request that Jesus would command that the two to whom she pointed (though Jesus knew them well enough!) should sit one at his right hand and the other at his left in his kingdom. We see here once again the general climate of incomprehension in which Jesus lived, for he had just told the disciples that he knew that he would be violently put to death at Jerusalem. He thus said to them first that they had no understanding. He concluded with the statement that is relevant for us: "You know that the rulers of the nations lord it over them, and those in high position enslave them. It shall not be so among you; but whoever would be great among you must be the servant." Note that he makes no distinction or reservation. All national rulers, no matter what the nation or the political regime, lord it over their subjects. There can be no political power without tyranny. This is plain and certain for Jesus. When there are rulers and great leaders, there can be no such thing as good political power. Here again power is called into question. Power corrupts. We catch an echo of the verse that we quoted above from Ecclesiastes. But we note also that Jesus does not advocate revolt or material conflict with these kings and great ones. He reverses the question, and as so often challenges his interlocutors: "But you . . . it must not be the same among you." In other words, do not be so concerned about fighting kings. Let them be. Set up a marginal society which will not be interested in such things, in which there will be no power, authority, or hierarchy.[7] Do not do things as they are usually done in society, which you cannot change. Create another society on another foundation.

We might condemn this attitude, talking of depoliticization. As we shall see, this was in fact the global attitude of Jesus. But we must take note that it is not desocialization. Jesus is not advising us to leave society and go into the desert. His counsel is that we should stay in society and set up in it communities which obey other rules and other laws. This advice rests on the conviction that we cannot change the phenomenon of power. And this is prophetic in a sense when we consider what became of the church when it entered the political field and began to play politics. It was immediately corrupted by the relation to power and by the creation of its own authorities. Finally, of course, one might rightly object that setting up independent communities outside the political power was relatively easy in the days of Jesus but is no longer possible today. This is a real objection but it is hardly enough to convince us that we may engage in politics, which is always a means of conquering others and exercising power over them.

---

7. One is always astounded, when reading sayings of this kind, that the church has been able to set up its own hierarchies, princes, and primates.

The third saying that I want to adduce concerns taxes again, and the question that is put is much the same as the one we have met already. We read in Matthew 17:24ff. that "when they came to Capernaum, the collectors of the half-shekel tax spoke to Peter and said, 'Does not your teacher pay the half-shekel tax?' Peter responded, 'Yes.' And when he came into the house, Jesus said to him, 'What do you think, Simon? From whom do the kings of the earth take tribute or taxes? From their own sons or from foreigners?' Peter answered, 'From foreigners.' Jesus then said to him, 'The sons are thus free. However, not to scandalize them, go to the lake, cast your line, and take the first fish that comes up. Open its mouth, and you will find a shekel; take that and give it to them for me and for yourself.'"

Naturally, for a long time attention focused on the "miracle." Jesus was making money like a magician! But the miracle is without real importance as such. On the contrary, we have to remember that the miracles of Jesus are quite different from marvels. He performs miracles of healing out of love and compassion. He performs some extraordinary miracles (e.g., stilling the storm) to come to the help of people. He never performs miracles to astonish people or to prove his power or to stir up belief in his divine sonship. He refuses to perform miracles on demand. If people say: Perform this miracle and we will believe in you, he refuses absolutely. (This is why faith is not linked to miracles!) A miracle of the type found here is thus inconceivable in and for itself. What then is the point of it?

Jesus first states that he does not owe the tax. The half-shekel tax was the temple tax. But it was not simply in aid of the priests. It was also levied by Herod the king. It was thus imposed for religious purposes but was taken over in part by the ruler. Jesus claims that he is a son, not merely a Jew but the Son of God. Hence he plainly does not owe this religious tax. Yet it is not worth causing offense for so petty a matter, that is, causing offense to the little people who raise the tax, for Jesus does not like to cause offense to the humble. He thus turns the matter into a subject of ridicule. That is the point of the miracle. The power which imposes the levy is ridiculous, and he thus performs an absurd miracle to show how unimportant the power is. The miracle displays the complete indifference of Jesus to the king, the temple authorities, etc. Catch a fish — any fish — and you will find the coin in its mouth. We find once again the typical attitude of Jesus. He devalues political and religious power. He makes it plain that it is not worth submitting and obeying except in a ridiculous way. One might object again that this was no doubt possible in his day but not now. At the same time it was an accumulation of little acts of this kind which turned the authorities against him and led to his crucifixion.

The fourth saying of Jesus concerns violence rather than political power. It is the well-known pronouncement: "All who take the sword will perish by the sword" (Matthew 26:52). The preamble to the saying presents a difficulty. According to Luke, Jesus surprisingly tells his disciples to buy swords. They have two, and Jesus tells them that is enough! The further comment of Jesus explains in part the surprising statement, for he says: "It is necessary that the prophecy be fulfilled according to which I would be put in the ranks of criminals" (Luke 22:36-37). The idea of fighting with just two swords is ridiculous. The two swords are enough, however, to justify the accusation that Jesus is the head of a band of brigands. We have to note here again that Jesus is consciously fulfilling prophecy. If he were not, the saying would make no sense.

But now let us take up the relevant saying which was uttered at the time of the arrest of Jesus. Peter was trying to defend his master. He wounded one of the guards. Jesus told him to stop, and in so doing uttered the celebrated saying which is an absolute judgment on everything that is based on violence. Violence can only give rise to further violence. An important point is that the saying is repeated in Revelation 13:10. The new and significant factor here is that the reference of the passage is to the beast that rises out of the sea. I have tried to show elsewhere that this beast represents political power in general and its various forms of force.[8] The beast that rises out of the earth is the equivalent of what we now call propaganda. The first beast, then, is the state, which uses violence and controls everything with no respect for human rights. It is face-to-face with this state that the author says: "Any one who kills with the sword will be killed by the sword." The meaning, of course, is ambivalent. On the one side, we might have here a cry of despair. Since the state uses the sword, it will be destroyed by the sword, as centuries of history have shown. But we might also view the saying as a command to Christians. Do not fight the state with the sword, for if you do, you will be killed by the sword. Again, therefore, we are oriented to nonviolence.

The trial of Jesus is the last episode in his life that we need to consider in this context. He was tried twice, once before the Sanhedrin and once before Pilate. Before going into his attitude, we must first deal with a preliminary question. Most theologians, including Karl Barth, take it that since Jesus agreed to appear before the jurisdiction of Pilate, showed respect for the authorities, and did not revolt against the verdict, this proves that he regarded the jurisdiction as legitimate, and we thus have here a basis for the power of the state. I have to say that I find this interpretation astounding, for I read the story in precisely the opposite way.

---

8. Cf. my *Apocalypse: The Book of Revelation* (New York: Seabury, 1977), pp. 92ff. See below for further explanation.

Pilate represents Roman authority and applies Roman law. Now, I concede that no civilization ever created so well-developed a law or could give such just decisions in trials, debates, and conflicts. I say this without irony. I taught Roman law for twenty years and discovered all the nuances and all the skill of jurists whose one aim was to say what was right. They defined law as the art of the good and the equitable, and I can guarantee that in hundreds of concrete cases they rendered decisions which showed that they were in effect dispensing justice. The Romans were not in the first instance ferocious fighters and conquerors, as they are often described. Their chief achievement was Roman law. A little problem which virtually no one considers is that their army, strictly speaking, was never large. At the most it seems to have had 120 legions, and these were nearly all stationed on the frontiers of the empire. They came into the interior only when there was a rebellion. The order of the empire was not a military order. It was through administrative skill and through the equilibrium established by skillful and satisfying legal measures that the empire endured for five centuries. We have to bear this in mind in evaluating what the accounts of the trial tell us.

The law of which the Romans were so proud and which provided the justest solutions — what did it accomplish in this instance? It allowed a Roman procurator to yield to the mob and to condemn an innocent man to death for no valid reason (as Pilate himself recognized!). This, then, is what we can expect from an excellent legal system! The fact that Jesus submits to the trial is not in these circumstances a recognition of the legitimacy of the authority of government. On the contrary, it is an unveiling of the basic injustice of what purports to be justice. This is what is felt when it is said that in the trial of Jesus all those who were condemned to death and crucified by the Romans are cleared. We thus find here once again the conviction of the biblical writers that all authority is unjust. We catch an echo of the saying of Ecclesiastes 3:16 that "where the seat of justice is found, there rules wickedness."⁹

Now let us look at the sayings and attitude of Jesus during the trial. There are differences among the four Gospels. The sayings are not exactly the same nor are they made before the same persons (at times the Sanhedrin, at times Herod, at times Caiaphas). But the attitude is always the same, whether it takes the form of silence, of accusation of the authorities, or of deliberate provocation. Jesus is not ready to debate, to excuse himself, or to recognize that these authorities have any real power. This is the striking point. I will take up in order the three aspects of his attitude.

First, there is silence. Before the chief priests and the whole Sanhedrin Jesus is silent. All the accounts agree that they sought witnesses against him, that they did not find any, but that finally two men said that he had stated that he would destroy the temple (Matthew 26:59-60). Jesus answered nothing. The authorities were astonished and ordered him to defend himself, but he remained silent. The same was true before Herod (recorded only in Luke 23:6ff.). Herod had him appear because he wanted to talk with him. But Jesus did not answer any of his questions. Before Pilate, Matthew and Mark tell us that he adopted the same attitude. This is the more surprising in view of the fact that Pilate could condemn him and he was not a priori unfavorably disposed to him. Many people were accusing him before Pilate. The chief priests brought many charges and Pilate asked him if he had no answer, but he did not reply (Matthew 27:12ff.). His attitude

9. The New Testament authors would obviously know the saying, for Ecclesiastes was solemnly read each year at the Feast of Sukkot (also called Booths or Tabernacles).

was one of total rejection and scorn for all religious or political authority. It seems that Jesus did not regard these authorities as in any way just and that it was thus completely useless to defend himself. From another point of view he took the offensive at times and manifested disdain or irony. Thus when asked whether he was the King of the Jews, according to two of the three accounts he made the ironical reply: "It is you who has said so" (Mark 15:2; Matthew 27:11). He himself would make no statement on the matter; they could say what they liked!

Second, his attitude involves accusation of the authorities. Thus he said to the chief priests: "I was with you every day in the temple, you did not lift a hand against me. But now you have come out with swords as against a brigand! Behold, your hour has come, and the power of darkness" (Luke 22:52-53). In other words, he expressly accused the chief priests of being an evil power. John records a similar episode (18:20-21) but with a different reply that is half irony and half accusation. When the high priest Annas asked him about his teaching, Jesus replied: "I have spoken openly to the world. Why do you question me? Question those who have heard me; they know what I said." When one of the officers struck him for this insolent answer, Jesus said to him: "If I have spoken wrongly, prove it; but if I have spoken rightly, why do you strike me?" Along the same lines of accusation there is another ambiguous text in John 19:10-11. Pilate said to Jesus: "You refuse to speak to me? Do you not know that I have power to free you or to have you crucified?" And Jesus replied: "You would not have the least power over me unless it had been given to you from above; therefore he who delivered me to you is more guilty than you."

The famous "from above" has been taken differently. Those who think that political power is from God find in it confirmation. Jesus is recognizing that Pilate has his power from God! But in this case I defy anyone to explain what is meant by the second part of his reply. How can the one who has delivered up Jesus be guilty if he has been delivered up to the authority which is from God? A second interpretation is purely historical. Jesus is saying to Pilate that his power was given him by the emperor. I have to say, though, that I can make no sense at all of this view. What point is there in Jesus telling Pilate that he depends on the emperor? What is the relevance of this to their discussion? Finally, there is the seldom advocated interpretation that I myself favor. Jesus is telling Pilate that his power is from the spirit of evil. This is in keeping with what we said about the temptations, namely, that all powers and kingdoms in this world depend on the devil. It is also in keeping with the reply of Jesus to the chief priests that we quoted above, namely, that the power of darkness is at work in his trial.

The second part of the saying is now easy to explain. Jesus is telling Pilate that he has his power from the spirit of evil but that the one who has delivered him up to Pilate, and therefore to that spirit, is more guilty than Pilate himself. Obviously so! If we accept the fact that these texts, which undoubtedly reproduce an oral tradition relating to the attitude of Jesus at the trial and probably contain his exact words, formulate the general opinion of the first Christian generation, why did the writers not state clearly that Pilate had his power from the spirit of evil? Why did they record so ambiguous a text? I think that the matter is simple enough. We must not forget that the Gospel was written at a time when Christians were coming under suspicion and when certain texts were put in code so that their meaning would not be clear!

Third, we find provocation on the part of Jesus. Thus when the high priest asked him whether he was the Messiah, the Son of God, he replied: "It is you who has said so," but he added: "Hereafter you will see the Son of man seated at the right hand of (divine) Power and coming on the clouds of heaven" (Matthew 26:64).[10] In relation to the whole theological teaching of the time, this is derisive. Jesus did not say that he was the Christ or that he would be at the right hand of Power. He did not say: "I." He said: "The Son of man." For those who are not very familiar with the Bible it must be pointed out that Jesus never said himself that he was the Christ (Messiah) or the Son of God. He always called himself the Son of man (i.e., true man). He was obviously mocking the high priest when he said: "Hereafter," that is, from the moment when *you* condemn me. (We find the same reply in Mark, and it seems to have been uttered by Jesus himself and handed down to the first Christian generation.)

Similar provocation is recorded in John 18:34ff., this time before Pilate. As so often happened, Jesus was trying to disconcert Pilate. When Pilate asked him: "Are you the King of the Jews" (v. 33), Jesus answered: "Do you say this of your own accord, or did others say it to you?" Pilate replied that he was not a Jew and that all he knew was that the Jewish authorities had handed Jesus over to him. He thus repeated the question, and this time Jesus made the ambiguous reply: "My kingship is not of this world [hence I am not competing with the emperor!]. If my kingship were of this world, my companions would have fought in order that I might not be handed over to the Jews." Pilate ignored these subtleties and insisted: "So you are king?" (This was the only charge on

10. The word "clouds" is often misunderstood. For the Jews the term "heaven," and especially "heaven of heavens," did not denote our blue sky with the moon and sun. Heaven is the dwelling place of God. It denotes what is inaccessible. "Heaven of heavens," an absolute superlative (i.e., heaven in the absolute), makes this point. As for the clouds, they simply denote the impossibility of knowing, of penetrating the mystery. They are the "veil." Painters who depict Jesus marching on the clouds are grossly mistaken.

which he could condemn Jesus.) Jesus, as we have seen already, answered: "It is you who has said so! [I myself have nothing to say on this subject.]" He then added: "I was born and I have come into this world to bear witness to the truth. Every one who is of the truth understands my word." Pilate then put his last question: "What is truth?" Jesus made no reply. He had no teaching to give to Pilate. Once again we find a kind of underlying mockery, a defiance or provocation of authority. Jesus spoke to Pilate in such a way as not to be understood.

In this lengthy series of texts relating to Jesus' face-to-face encounters with the political and religious authorities, we find irony, scorn, noncooperation, indifference, and sometimes accusation. Jesus was no guerrilla. He was an "essential" disputer.

3. Revelation

We shall now try to find out what was the attitude of the first Christian generations to power. We begin with Revelation.[11] This is one of the most violent texts, and it follows the sayings of Jesus but with even greater severity. It obviously has Rome in view, but not simply the presence of the Romans in Judea. At issue is the central imperial power of Rome itself. Throughout the book there is radical opposition between the majesty of God and the powers and dominions of earth. This shows how mistaken are those who find continuity between the divine power and earthly powers, or who argue, as under a monarchy, that a single earthly power ought to correspond to the one almighty God who reigns in heaven.

11. Cf. my *Apocalypse*, which shows that Revelation is not just a book of dramas and disasters.

Revelation teaches the exact opposite. The whole book is a challenge to political power.

I will simply mention two great symbols. The first is that of the two beasts. It takes up a theme of the later prophets, who depicted the political powers of their time as beasts. The first beast comes up from the sea. This probably represents Rome, whose armies came by sea. It has a throne that is given to it by the dragon (chs. 12–13). The dragon, anti-God, has given all authority to the beast. People worship it. They ask who can fight against it. It is given "all authority and power over every tribe, every people, every tongue, and every nation" (13:7). All who dwell on earth worship it. Political power could hardly, I think, be more expressly described, for it is this power which has authority, which controls military force, and which compels adoration (i.e., absolute obedience). This beast is created by the dragon. We thus find the same relation as that already noted between political power and the *diabolos*. Confirmation of this idea that the beast is the state may be found in the fact that at the end of Revelation (ch. 18) great Babylon (i.e., Rome) is destroyed. The beast unites all the kings of earth to make war on God and is finally crushed and condemned after his main representative has first been destroyed.

The second beast rises out of the earth. Specialists have railed against my interpretation of this beast, but I stand by it. It is described as follows. "It makes all the inhabitants of the earth worship the first beast. . . . It seduces the inhabitants of the earth. It tells them to make an image of the first beast. . . . It animates the image of the beast and speaks in its name. . . . It causes all, small and great, rich and poor, free and slave, to receive a mark on their right hand or on their forehead, so that no one can buy or sell without having the mark of the beast" (13:12-17). For my part, I find here an exact description of propaganda in association with the police. The beast makes speeches which induce people to obey the state, to worship it. It gives them the mark that enables them to live in society. Finally, those that will not obey the first beast are put to death.

The point is clear enough, I think. One of the main instruments of Roman propaganda was the establishment of the cult of Rome and the emperor with altars, temples, etc. The Jewish kings of the period accepted this. This is why the text speaks of the beast that rises up out of the earth. The local authorities in the provinces of the Near East were the most enthusiastic promoters of the cult of Rome. This was a kind of power that works on the intelligence and on credibility to obtain voluntary obedience to the beast. But let us not forget that for the Jews who wrote this text the state and its propaganda are two powers that derive from evil.

My second and last symbol is the fall of Great Babylon in ch. 18. There is general agreement that Babylon represents Rome. But it is also clear in the text that Rome is equated with supreme political power. All nations have drunk the wine of the fury of their vices. The first interesting feature is that of the fury or violence in evil. All the kings of the earth are delivered up to adultery. Political power is the climax, for earthly kings all lie with it. Merchants are enriched by the power of Babylon's luxury. The state is a means by which to concentrate wealth and it enriches its clients. We see the same thing today in the form of public works and arms production. Political power makes alliance with the power of money. When Babylon collapses, all the kings of the earth lament and despair and the capitalists weep. A long list is then given of the goods bought and sold at Rome, but the interesting point is that at the end of the list we find that great Babylon bought and sold human bodies and souls. If the reference were only to bodies we might think of slaves. But there is also a more general reference to souls. The slave trade is not the issue here. The point is that political authorities have all power over people. What is promised is the pure and simple destruction of political government: Rome, to be sure, yet not Rome alone, but power and domination in every form. These things are specifically stated to be enemies of God. God judges political power, calling it the great harlot. We can expect from it neither justice, nor truth, nor any good — only destruction.

At this point, as may be seen, we are far from the rebellion of Jesus against Roman colonization. As Christians became more numerous and Christian thought developed, the Christian view of political power hardened. Only reductionist thinking can see this passage as directed solely against Rome. The hardening might be due to the beginning of persecution, of which the text gives evidence, for the great harlot "was drunk with the blood of saints and with the blood of witnesses to Jesus." "In the great city was found the blood of prophets and of saints, of all who had been slain on earth" (18:24). (The reference, of course, is to the slaying not merely of the first Christians but of all the righteous.) A remarkable point is that according to 20:4 those who were thus put to death for their Christian allegiance were beheaded. They were not killed in the arena or fed to lions, etc. Power slays not merely Christians but all righteous people. This experience undoubtedly strengthened the conviction that political power would be condemned. I believe that among the first Christians there was no other global position. At this period Christianity was totally hostile to the state.

4. 1 Peter

Before taking a look at Paul we must glance at a strange passage in a later epistle, namely, 1 Peter 2:13ff., which tells us to "be subject to the king as supreme" and to "honor the king." Oddly, this passage has never given commentators any difficulty. As they see it, the matter is simple enough. The king was the Roman emperor. That is all. On this basis, then, sermons are preached on the obedience and submission of Christians to political authorities. Interestingly, in parallel Bibles there is usually a cross-reference to the saying of Jesus that we must render to Caesar what is Caesar's. In fact, however, this whole line of exposition displays great ignorance regarding the political institutions of the period.

First, the head of the Roman state was then the *princeps*. This was the term for the emperor at the time when the Christian texts were written. The period is known historically as the principate. The *princeps* was never called the king (Greek *basileus*). The title was formally forbidden in Rome. We have to realize that Caesar was assassinated on the rumored charge that he was planning to restore the monarchy. That was a good enough reason. Augustus was careful enough never to hint at anything of this kind. He acted very cleverly, simply assuming successively the republican titles of "consul," "people's tribune," and "commander in chief" (*imperator*, which should not be translated "emperor"). He then took also the title of "supreme pontiff," exercising religious functions. All these were traditional titles of Rome's democracy. Augustus also took steps to abolish "abnormal" institutions that had arisen during the civil war, for example, the triumvirate and the permanent consulate, and he opposed the creation of a dictatorship. Having taken all power to himself, he was content with the title *princeps* or first citizen. The people alone was sovereign, and it delegated its *potestas* to the *princeps*. This delegation was by a regular procedure. To avoid military coups, Augustus had the plenitude of power assigned to the senate by a democratic vote. He then received some imprecise titles without legal content, for example, "father of the country," "guardian of the citizens" *(servator civium)*. He was also *princeps senatus,* first senator. He restored the regular functioning of republican institutions. His successors were less scrupulous than he was. Little by little they established the empire, but never in an absolute and totalitarian sense. And they never took the title "king." They expressly avoided any reference to this title or any assigning of it to themselves. Hence the author of 1 Peter can hardly have had the emperor in view in this passage.

I thus want to make a hazardous suggestion. What follows is pure hypothesis. There were political parties at Rome. During the 1st century a strange party evolved on the basis of a global philosophy. This philosophy was as follows. The world's empires have a cyclical life. A political power is born, grows, reaches its height, and then, unable to grow further, inevitably declines, entering a period of decomposition. This applied to all known empires. Hence it applied to Rome as well. Many writers of the 1st century thought that Rome had already reached the summit of its power. Its rule stretched from Spain to Persia, from Scotland to the Sahara and the south of Egypt. It could not expand any more. In consequence its decline was beginning. After the period of glorification and enthusiasm such as we see in Vergil and Livy, there thus came a period of dark pessimism among less well-known writers and philosophers. It should be added that whenever one empire collapsed (e.g., Egypt, Babylon, or Persia), a new one arose to take its place. In all probability this would also happen in the case of Rome. But the Parthians were the only unconquered enemy of Rome, and they were constantly invading new territories. One group, first of intellectuals, then of members of the governing class, very seriously envisioned the Roman empire being replaced by a Parthian empire. Some of them, entering into the flow of history, began to spread these ideas and founded, it is said, a party that would finally support the Parthians.

Now the Parthians, for their part, were governed by a king. Some think that prayers were being said for the king, that is, the Parthian king, and that they were forbidden. If we grant this, and some historians, of course, dispute it, the text in 1 Peter is seen in a new light. There can be no question of honoring the emperor under the name of king, or of praying for the king of Rome! But Peter twice refers to the king. Why, then, should he not have had the Parthian king in view? If so, the passage is a totally subversive one. But the reference in this case is solely to the political power of Rome and not to the state as such, for the author is supporting another power. Nevertheless, the passage is in accord with the general Christian attitude, which is far from being one of passivity or obedience, and which we might classify in three ways.

1. It may be first an attitude of scorn, of a refusal to recognize the validity of political power, though not of total rejection.
2. It may be an attitude of total repudiation of political power.
3. It may be an attitude of condemnation of Roman power. After the capture of Jerusalem by the Roman armies, the destruction of the temple, the suppression of the autonomy of Jewish government, the massacre of thousand of Jews during the war, and finally the suppression of the Christian church at Jerusalem in A.D. 70, the Christian hatred of political power clearly came to focus on Rome.

5. Paul

We finally arrive at the passages in Paul. We had first to fix the general Christian climate in order to put the verses in context. Although they are (too!) well known, I will quote them. First we have Romans 13:1-7: "Let every person be subject to the higher authorities. For there is no authority which does not come from God, and the authorities that exist have been instituted by God. Therefore the one who resists authority resists the order that God has established, and those who resist will bring condemnation on themselves. It is not for good conduct but for bad that magistrates are to be feared. The magistrate is the servant of God for your good. But if you do evil, be afraid, for it is not in vain that he bears the sword, being the servant of God to exercise vengeance and punish those who do evil. It is necessary therefore to be subject, not only for fear of punishment but also for the sake of conscience. It is also for this reason that you pay taxes, for the magistrates are servants of God, attending entirely to this function. Pay to all of them what is their due, taxes to whom you owe taxes, tribute to whom you owe tribute, fear to whom you owe fear, honor to whom you owe honor." We then have Titus 3:1: "Remind them to be subject to magistrates and authorities, to obey and to be ready for any good work."

These are the only texts in the whole Bible which stress obedience and the duty of obeying the authorities. It is true that two other passages show that there was among Christians of the time a counterflow to the main current that we have demonstrated. In 2 Peter 2:10 there is condemnation of those who "despise authority," and Jude 8 also condemns those who "carried along by their dreamings . . . despise authority, and revile the glorious ones." We must emphasize, however, that these are very ambiguous texts. What is the authority that they have in view? We must never forget the constant reminder that all authority belongs to God.

Finally, we might adduce 1 Timothy 2:1-2: "Therefore I exhort that, above all things, make prayers, supplications, petitions, and thanksgivings for all humans, for kings, and for all who are in high positions, that we may lead a peaceable and quiet life in all reverence and honesty."

In these Pauline texts we seem to have a trend that differs from the one we have just seen. Our next task is to pose a completely incomprehensible (or, alas! only too comprehensible) problem. From the 3rd century A.D. most theologians, simply forgetting all that we have shown, have focused solely on the statements of Paul in Romans 13 and preached total submission to authority. They have done this without taking into account (as we have done) the context of the statements. They have even fixed on one statement in particular: "All power comes from God." This has been the leading theme in sixteen centuries of cooperation between church and state: *omnis potestas a Deo*. Some bold theologians added *per populum* (by way of the people), but this was a mere detail as compared to the imperious duty of obeying the power that is from God as though it were itself God.

The curious thing is to see how theologians fared when often to their embarrassment they had to do with tyrants. A strange casuistry was adopted to explain that power comes from God only when it is gained in a legal, legitimate, and peaceful way and exercised in a moral and regular way. But this did not call into question the general duty. Even at the time of the Reformation Luther used this text in the Peasants' War to charge the princes to crush the revolt. As for Calvin, he insisted that kings are legitimate except when they attack the church. So long as the authorities let Christians freely practice their religion, they cannot be faulted. As I see it, we have here an incredible betrayal of the original Christian view, and the source of this betrayal is undoubtedly the tendency toward conformity and the ease of obeying. However that may be, the only rule that has been gathered from the vast array of texts is that there is no authority except from

God. We shall now try to examine the Pauline passages more closely.

As in the case of all biblical texts (and all other texts!) we must first refuse to detach one phrase from the total line of thinking. We must put that phrase in the general context. Let us, then, take Paul's argument as a whole. In Romans 9–11 Paul has just made a detailed study of the relations between the Jewish people and Christians. A new development then begins which will cover chs. 12–14 and at the heart of which is the passage that we are now considering. This lengthy discussion begins with the words: "Do not be conformed to the present age but be transformed by the renewal of your mind." Paul's general and essential command, then, is that we should not be conformists, that we should not obey the trends and customs and currents of thought of the society in which we live, that we should not submit to the "form" of them but that we should be transformed, that we should receive a new form by the renewing of the mind, that is, by starting from a new point, namely, the will of God and love. This is obviously a strange beginning if he is later to demand obedience to political authorities! Paul then goes on to teach at length about love: love among Christians in the church (12:3-8), love for all people (12:9-13), and love for enemies (not avenging oneself, but blessing those who persecute), with a further exhortation to live peaceably with all (12:14-21). The passage on the authorities follows next. Then all the commandments are summed up in the commandment of love and of doing no wrong to others (13:8-10). In ch. 14 some details are offered as to the practice of love (hospitality, not judging others, supporting the weak, etc.).

This, then, is the general framework or movement within which the passage on authority occurs. It seems so odd, so out of joint, in this larger context that some exegetes have thought that it must be an interpolation and that Paul himself did not write it. For my part, however, I believe that it has its place here and that it does come from the apostle. We have seen that there is a progression of love from friends to strangers and then to enemies, and this is where the passage then comes. In other words, we must love enemies and therefore we must even respect the authorities, not loving them but accepting their orders. We have to remember that the authorities have attained to power through God. Yes, we recall that Saul, a mad and bad king, attained to power through God. This certainly does not mean that he was good, just, or lovable. Along the same lines one of the best commentators on the passage, Alphonse Maillot, relates it directly to the end of ch. 12: "Do not let yourself be overcome by evil, but overcome evil with good. Let every person (therefore) be subject to the higher authorities...." In other words, Paul belongs to that Christian church which at the first is unanimously hostile to the state, to the imperial power, to the authorities, and in this text he is thus moderating that hostility. He is reminding Christians that the authorities are also people (there was no abstract concept of the state), people such as themselves, and that they must accept and respect them, too. At the same time Paul shows great restraint in this counsel. When he tells them to pay their dues — taxes to whom taxes are due, revenue to whom revenue, respect to whom respect, honor to whom honor — we are rightly reminded of the answer of Jesus regarding the tax. Far more boldly Jesus claims that we owe neither respect nor honor to magistrates or the authorities. The only one whom we must fear is God. The only one to whom honor is due is God. (In an appendix I will adduce two of the better commentaries on this passage.)

Three points still call for discussion. The first presents no difficulty. We have met it already. It relates to the paying of taxes. Christians must not refuse to pay them. That is all.

The second is more striking: We must pray for the authorities. We have quoted the passage in which Paul asks that prayer be made for kings — the plural shows that we cannot expound this as we did in the case of 1 Peter — namely, for those in authority, for the government. This verse confirms what I said above. Paul is saying in effect that we are to pray for all people. Included are kings and those in high office. We are to pray even for kings and magistrates. We detest them, but we are still to pray for them. No one must be excluded from our intercession, from our appeal to God's love for them. It might seem completely crazy, but I knew some German Christians who were in the resistance movement against Hitler, even to the point of plotting his overthrow, and who still engaged in prayer for him.[12] We cannot want the absolute death of political foes. Certainly our prayer will not be a kind of Te Deum. It will not be prayer that they remain in power, that they win victories, that they endure. It will be prayer for their conversion, that they change the way they behave and act, that they renounce violence and tyranny, that they become truthful, etc. Yet we still pray *for* them and not against them. In Christian faith we will also pray for their salvation (which is obviously not the same thing as the safety of their kingdom). This prayer must still be made even if from a human standpoint there is no hope of change. We must not forget that these passages on respect and prayer were probably written at the very moment of the first persecution under Nero, or shortly after it. We thus have to say to Christians, as Paul does in Romans 13, that even though you are revolted by persecutions, even though you are ready to rebel, instead pray for the authorities. Your only

12. It is not out of place to recall that the only ones to organize resistance to Hitler after 1936 were German Protestants of the Confessing Church.

true weapon is to turn to God, for it is he alone who dispenses supreme justice.

We now come to the final point. I cannot close these reflections on this passage, which unfortunately gave a wrong turn to the church and Christianity after the 3rd century, without recalling a study of some thirty years ago.[13] The word used in this train of thought is in Greek *exousiai,* which can mean the public authorities, but which has also in the New Testament another meaning, being used for abstract, spiritual, religious powers. Thus Paul tells us that we are to fight against the *exousiai* enthroned in heaven (cf. Eph. 6:12). It is thought, for example, that the angels are *exousiai.* Oscar Cullmann and Günther Dehn thus conclude that since the same word is used there has to be some relation.[14] In other words, the New Testament leads us to suppose that earthly political and military authorities really have their basis in an alliance with spiritual powers, which I will not call celestial, since they might equally well be evil and demonic. The existence of these spiritual *exousiai* would explain the universality of political powers and also the astonishing fact that people obey them as though it were self-evident. These spiritual authorities would then inspire rulers.

Now these authorities might be either good or bad, angelic or demonic. Earthly authorities reflect the powers into whose hands they have fallen. We can thus see why Paul in Romans 13 refers to the authorities that actually "exist" as being instituted by God and also why some Protestant

13. See O. Cullmann, *Heil als Geschichte* (Tübingen: Mohr, 1965); Eng. trans. *Salvation in History* (Naperville: Allenson, 1967).
14. See ibid.; idem, *Christ and Time,* 3rd ed. (London: SCM, 1962), pp. 193ff.; idem, *The State in the New Testament* (New York: Scribner's, 1956), pp. 93ff.; G. Dehn, "Engel und Obrigkeit: Ein Beitrag zum Verständnis von Römer 13, 1-7," in *Theologische Aufsätze für Karl Barth* (Munich: Christian Kaiser, 1936), pp. 90-109.

theologians could say after 1933 that Hitler's was a "de-monized" state which had fallen into the hands of a demonic power. If I say this, it is not simply because I want to say that the attitude of the first Christian generation was not abso-lutely unanimous, that alongside the main line, according to which the state should be destroyed, there was a more nuanced line (though no one demanded unconditional obe-dience). The important point for me is that when Paul in Colossians 2:13-15 says that Jesus has conquered evil and death he also says that Christ has "stripped of their power all the dominions and authorities and made a public spec-tacle of them, in triumphing over them by the cross." In Christian thinking the crucifixion of Christ is his true victory over all powers both celestial and infernal (I am not saying whether they exist but expressing the conviction of the day), for he alone has been perfectly obedient to the will of God, even accepting the scandal of his own condemnation and execution (without fully understanding it: "My God, why have you abandoned me?"). Though he has doubts about his interpretation and mission, he has no doubts about the will of God and he obeys perfectly.

I know how scandalous for non-Christians is a God who demands this death. But the real question is this: How far can love go? Who will love God so absolutely as to lose himself? This was the test (stopped in time) for Abraham. It was also the test that provoked the anger of Job. But Jesus alone obeyed to the very end (when he was fully free not to obey!). For that reason, having loved beyond human limits, he robbed the powers of their power! Demons no longer hold sway. There are not independent *exousiai*. All are from the very outset subject to Christ. They may revolt, of course, but they are overcome in advance. Politically this means that the *exousia* which exists alongside or outside political power is also vanquished. The result is that political power is not a final court. It is always relative. We can expect from it only what is relative and open to question. This is the meaning of Paul's statement and it shows how much we need to relativize the (traditionally absolutized) formula that there is no authority except from God. Power is indeed from God, but all power is overcome in Christ!

Appendixes

THE INTERPRETATION OF ROMANS 13:1-2
BY KARL BARTH AND ALPHONSE MAILLOT

I will present in summary fashion two interpretations by two important authors so as to show that all theologians and the whole church have not been unanimous in interpreting this passage as an absolute truth in the matter of the state. We must still recognize, of course, that it is a very embarrassing passage.

1. Karl Barth

In his great commentary on the Epistle to Romans which was his theological manifesto in 1919,[1] Barth begins his exposition

1. Karl Barth, *Der Römerbrief,* 1st ed. (Bern: G. A. Bäschlin, 1919); 2nd ed. (Munich: Christian Kaiser, 1922); Eng. trans. of 2nd ed., *The Epistle to the Romans* (London: Oxford, 1933; 6th ed. repr. 1980).

of Romans 13:1ff. by agreeing that order is indispensable for societies and that political institutions are part of this order. We should not wrongly or arbitrarily overthrow the order. The passage thus counsels nonrevolution, but in so doing, by that very fact, it also teaches the intrinsic nonlegitimacy of institutions. All established order presents those who seek God's order with triumphant injustice. The issue is not the evil quality of the order but the fact that it is established. This is what wounds the desire for justice. In these conditions every authority becomes a tyranny. Nevertheless, revolutionaries are in fact overcome by evil. For they, too, claim to represent intrinsic justice. In so doing they usurp a legitimacy that will at once become a tyranny (written in 1919!). Evil is no answer to evil. The sense of justice that is offended by the established order is not restored by the destruction of the order. Revolutionaries have in view the impossible possibility: truth, justice, forgiveness of sins, brotherly love, the resurrection of the dead. But they achieve another revolution, the possible possibility of hatred, revenge, and destruction. They dream of the true revolution but launch the other. The text is not favoring what is established but rejecting all human enemies of what is established. For God alone wills to be acknowledged as the victor over the injustice of what is established.

As for the exhortation to submit to the authorities, it is purely negative. It means withdrawal, nonparticipation, noninvolvement. Even if revolution is always a just condemnation of what is established, this is not due to any sense to the act of the rebels. The conflict into which rebels plunge is the conflict between the order of God and what is established. Rebels finally establish an order which bears the same features as the preceding order. They ought to be converted instead of rebelling. The fact that we must submit means that we should not forget how wrong political calculation is as such.

[87]

The revelation of God bears witness to true justice. We could not more effectively undermine what is established than by recognizing it as we are here commanded. For state, church, society, positive justice, and science all live on the credulity which is nurtured by the enthusiasm of chaplains and solemn humbug. Deprive these institutions of their pathos and they will die of starvation. (We find here the same orientation as that uncovered in the attitude of Jesus.) Non-revolution is the best preparation for the true revolution (which for Barth is that of the will of God and the kingdom of God).

Barth finally comes to the text, for which all of the above is introductory. Only in appearance, he says, does the text provide a basis for order. For all authority, like everything else that is human, is measured by God, who is at the same time its beginning and end, its justification and condemnation, its Yes and its No. God is the sole criterion that enables us to grasp that the bad at the heart of what is established is really bad. Hence we have no right to claim God in validation of this order as if he were at our service. It is before God alone that what is established falls. The text sets what is established in God's presence. This takes away all the pathos, justification, illusion, enthusiasm, etc. Very freely Barth quotes 12:10. Setting up justice is God's affair. Submitting, then, is recognizing the strict authority of God alone. Through not paying heed to this for so many centuries, the churches have betrayed the cause of humanity by deferring to the state. The true revolution can come from God alone. Human revolutionaries claim that they can bring a new cre-ation and create a new, good, brotherly humanity, but in so doing they fail to see the sole justice (and justification) of God and the order that God alone can and will set up in opposition to established human order.

2. Alphonse Maillot

Although not a theologian of the stature of Karl Barth, Maillot is one of the best living commentators on the Bible.[2] He offers a different perspective from that of Barth. He begins with a very astute question. Throughout his writings Paul is against legalism. He shows that the Torah is marginal. The only law is that of love. The work of Jesus is one of liberation. How, then, can he become a legalist and a champion of law when it is a matter of social and political institutions?

What Paul shows is on the one side that the political structure is not outside the will of God and that it cannot prevent us from obeying God. If the state threatens to enmesh us in evil, then we must reject it. Paul rejects all Manichaeism, all dualism. There cannot be a world in which some things are not in God's hand. Rulers, magistrates, etc. — they, too, are in God's hand in spite of their pretensions.

Paul also speaks of authorities that actually exist. He is referring, says Maillot, to those of his own day. He does not legislate for all history. The duty of Christians is to bear witness to what they believe to be the truth. It is because we believe that the authorities are in God's hand that we have the possibility (seldom utilized) of telling them what we think is just. If Paul also tells us that we are to obey, not by constraint but for the sake of conscience, this means that our obedience can never be blind or resigned. For conscience might lead us to disobey, obeying God rather than humans, as Peter says (Acts 5:29). This would be for reasons that politicians cannot understand.[3]

2. Alphonse Maillot, *L'Epître aux Romains* (Geneva: Labor et Fides, 1984).

3. In typical fashion Maillot shows that a military law of conscientious objection is absurd. It is a contradiction in terms. Objectors are obeying conscience; military law aims at the smooth functioning of the military machine. There can be no mutual understanding.

Finally, Maillot's most important point is as follows. Paul wrote this when he had already been imprisoned several times. He did not take politicians for choirboys. He would shortly afterward be executed by the Roman authorities. His difficult life and death "delegalize" ch. 13.

Maillot also puts the chapter in the general context of the epistle, but in a different way from mine, since he covers a wider field. As he sees it, the letter as a whole seeks to show the movement of God's saving righteousness in human history. Paul wants to demonstrate this in every aspect of human reality. The church and Israel (about which Paul speaks prior to ch. 13) are not the only ones to make history. There are also politics and human society. Paul seeks to show that the *polis* is also part of God's plan, that it is not alien to his will, that it can have a part in his saving righteousness. It seems, says Maillot, that the meeting between Christians and non-Christians was inevitable at times when a pagan magistrate became a Christian. Could one be a judge and a Christian or a tax collector and a Christian? Paul indeed speaks to members of the praetorian guard (Philippians 1:13) and Caesar's household (4:22). Undoubtedly, with the tasks they had to perform these Roman officials who were also Christians had to face spiritual difficulties!

Maillot also emphasizes concretely what we pointed out earlier, namely, the general opposition of the first Christians to power. Paul, then, wants to "compensate." Civil structures, the magistrates, and even Nero are integrated into the dynamism of the righteousness of God, though not in the same way as Israel and the church. Ultimately, they are not from the devil but from God. Christians, then, must not repudiate them. At the same time Paul is not answering the question posed by a regime that tips over into the demonic. His point is that magistrates ought to support the good. If, then, they become flagrant supporters of evil, we have to review our relation to them. In any case true obedience is not just a copy of other obedience!

CONSCIENTIOUS OBJECTORS

Thus far I have been investigating the biblical texts which express, as I have said, the opinion or orientation of the first Christian generation. We do not have here purely individual witness or opinion, for we should not forget that these texts became "holy scripture" only as they were regarded as such by the majority in the church (not by a council but by grass-roots consensus). We shall now take a look at the application of these orientations by Christians in the first three centuries who became "rebel citizens."[4]

Before studying the main point of conflict, the question of conscientious objection, we need to look first at some by no means negligible factors. In the 2nd century Celsus in his *True Word,* among other criticisms of Christianity, described Christians as enemies of the human race. He did so because they opposed the Roman order, the *pax Romana.* This meant that they hated the human race, which was organized by Rome. Later, when Christianity had ceased to be a little sect and had become an aggressive religion, Christians were accused of weakening the empire by their contempt for magistrates and military leaders. This was one of the complaints of Julian the Apostate. It was the fault of Christians that Roman organization was crumbling and that the Roman army had lost many frontier wars. Julian advanced an argument that does not seem valid to us today, namely, that Christians led people no longer to respect and serve the traditional city gods and that these had abandoned Rome, so that Rome had now became decadent. Return to the an-

---

4. In this section I am simply summarizing the remarkable work of Jean-Michel Hornus, *It Is Not Lawful for Me to Fight: Early Christian Attitudes Toward War, Violence, and the State,* rev. ed. (Scottdale, PA: Herald, 1980).

cient gods, and Rome will recover its greatness. We can ignore that argument, but what historians of the later empire all agree on is that the Christians were not interested in political matters or military ventures.

There are two sides to this. On the one hand, for centuries Roman intellectuals had been passionately interested in law and in the organization of the city and the empire. But after the 3rd century they become passionately interested in theology. On the other hand, Christians were not willing to function as magistrates or officials. So long as Christianity was winning over only the lower social classes — and it spread first among the city poor, among freedmen and slaves — that did not greatly matter. But as it made inroads into the rich and governing classes, the defection became serious. Many documents show how hard it became to recruit *curiales* (mayors) for cities, governors for provinces, and military officers, because Christians refused to hold such offices. They were not concerned about the fate of society. When the emperor tried to force them to become *curiales,* many of them preferred to retire to their secondary residences in the country and to live as landed proprietors. As for the army, the emperor had to recruit foreign (barbarian) officers. Some modern historians think that this general defection on the part of Christians was one of the most important reasons for the decline of Rome from the 4th century onwards.

We now return to Christian practice prior to the 3rd century. It was dominated by the thinking of Tertullian, who, after proving that the church and empire are necessarily anti-Christian and therefore hostile to God, seems to have been one of the first to champion total conscientious objection. One of his fine phrases is that the Caesars would have been Christians if it were possible to have Christian Caesars or if Caesars were not necessary for the world (i.e., the world in the New Testament sense as the epitome of what is inimical to God). This said, the practical point at which opposition expressed itself (apart from refusal to worship the emperor) was military service.

Historians have debated heavily this matter of military service. A few inscriptions show that there were some Christian soldiers, but only a few (and these perhaps conscripted). It is fairly certain that up to A.D. 150 soldiers who became Christians did all they could to leave the army, and Christians did not enlist in it. The number of Christian soldiers would grow in the second half of the 3rd century in spite of the disapproving attitude of the church authorities and the whole Christian community.[5] But even though there were more Christian soldiers, they caused trouble. Thus one soldier refused to put on the official laurel wreath at an official ceremony. On another occasion Diocletian made an offering with a view to knowing the future *(haruspice),* and when the sacrifice failed, the failure was blamed on some Christian soldiers who made the sign of the cross. One might say that military service had become a fact by A.D. 250, but through conscription and not by choice. From the end of the 2nd century emphasis was placed on the example of soldier martyrs, that is, those who were recruited by force but who absolutely refused to serve and were put to death as a result. This happened in time of war. It is recorded that some soldiers who were chosen to execute their comrades suddenly decided on conversion and threw down their swords. Numerous examples are given by Lactantius and Tertullian.

It is possible, then, to speak of a massive Christian antimilitarism. The *Apostolic Tradition* of Hippolytus, an official collection of church rules at the beginning of the 3rd century, says that those who have the power of the sword or

5. See E. A. Ryan, "The Rejection of Military Service by the Early Christians," *Theological Studies* 13 (1952) 1-32.

who are city magistrates must leave their offices or be dismissed from the church. If catechumens or believers want to become soldiers they must be dismissed from the church, for they are despising God. In these conditions the number of Christians who were executed rose, the period of massive persecution began, and what came to be known as "soldier saints" were created.

A slight change came with the Council of Elvira in 313, which merely ruled that those who held a peaceful office in the administration should not be allowed to enter the church while holding office. What was condemned was all participation in power that implied coercion. At this time also (ca. 312-313) came the conversion of Constantine. Though the legend is familiar, his conversion was probably a matter of political calculation. Due to their numbers Christians had now become a by no means negligible political force and Constantine had need of all the support he could muster to gain power. The general populace as well as intellectuals and the aristocracy was abandoning the ancient religions. There was a religious void, and Constantine knew how to exploit it. He officially adopted Christianity and in so doing trapped the church, which readily let itself be trapped, being largely led at this time by a hierarchy drawn from the aristocracy. Some theologians tried to resist. As late as the end of the 4th century Basil said that to kill in war is murder and that soldiers who had engaged in combat should be refused communion for three years. Since war was permanent, this meant permanent excommunication. But this had now become the view merely of a small body of resisters. The fact that Christianity was becoming the official religion, and that the churches would receive great privileges, won over most of the leaders.

Thus at the Synod of Arles in 314, summoned by the emperor himself, the teaching on administrative and military service was completely reversed. The third canon of the council excommunicated soldiers who refused military service or who mutinied. The seventh canon permitted Christians to be state officials, requiring only that they not take part in pagan acts (e.g., emperor worship), and that they observe the church's discipline (e.g., abstaining from all murderous violence). Some expositors think that the Council of Arles forbade killing, but if so, it is hard to see what the role of soldiers could be. In reality the state had begun to dominate the church and to obtain from it what was in basic contradiction with its original thinking. With this council the antistatist, antimilitarist, and, as we should now say, anarchist movement of Christianity came to an end.

TESTIMONY: PRIEST AND ANARCHIST

For twenty years I have been serving as priest and pastor in a parish of 2,000 inhabitants. I also work three days a week in a metal construction company. I am known to many people here as an anarchist. I am asked how I can reconcile my position as both a Christian and an anarchist. I not only feel no opposition between my Christian faith and my anarchist convictions but my knowledge of Jesus of Nazareth impels me toward anarchism and gives me courage to practice it.

"No God, no Master" and "I believe in God the Father Almighty" — these two convictions I hold in all sincerity. No one can be the master of others in the sense of being superior. No one can impose his or her will on others. I do not know God at all as supreme Master.

I reject all human hierarchy. Jean-Paul Sartre finely expressed the unique value of every human being when he said that one human being, no matter who, is of equal worth to all others. Before Sartre, Jesus made no distinction between people. Those in power were upset by his attitude and wanted his death. They said to him: "You speak without worrying about what will be, for you do not regard the position of persons" (Matthew 22:16). Human life transcends all the laws that try to organize society. Matthew, Mark, Luke, and John are full of stories of clashes between Jesus and the authorities because he violated the law out of concern for individual lives.

It is in this spirit that we have collected a number of signatures in favor of freedom of movement, stating that Elena Bonner, wife of Sakharov, ought to be able to go to the West if she judges that to be necessary to her health, and that people in the South ought to be free to go to countries in the North if they think this to be vitally necessary.

I reject hierarchy between us and God. God, at least the

[96]

God whom Jesus calls Father and whom he tells us to call Father, is never presented to us as a Master who imposes his will on us or who regards us as inferiors. For Jesus there is no hierarchical relation between Father and Son. He says: "I and the Father are one . . . he in me and I in him" (cf. John 10:30; 17:21).

Religious people who can think only in terms of rivalry, superiority, equality, and inferiority thus bring against Jesus the charge that he is making himself God's equal. They are incapable of imagining that a man, Jesus, can be God with his Father, and that the vocation of all of us is to be God with the Father.

The author of Genesis (to refer to the Bible) finds our human fault in this attitude of wanting to become as gods knowing good and evil instead of being with God in enjoyment of life and the pleasure of creating life. That attitude of those who are preoccupied with themselves and their rank engenders every kind of unhappiness. We are left alone, naked and scornful, mutually accusing one another, toiling for ourselves, in creation and procreation sowing death, fighting for domination or accepting domination in fear.

The prophets unceasingly tell us to live in covenant with God, but under the sway of the authorities we prefer to assert ourselves by attacking others.

Look at 1 Samuel 8 in the Bible. The elders of Israel said to Samuel: "Give us a king to govern us." God then said to Samuel: "Give satisfaction to the people for all that they ask. . . . They have rejected me because they do not want me to reign over them." Samuel then told the people what God had said: "This will be the status of the king who will reign over you: he will take your sons and appoint them to his chariots and to be his horsemen and to run before his chariot. He will use them as commanders of thousands and commanders of fifties; he will make them labor and harvest to his profit, to make his implements of war and his harnesses. He will take your daughters for the preparation of his perfumes and for his bakery. He will take the best of your fields, your vineyards, and your olive orchards and give them to his servants. He will take the tenth of your grain and of your vineyards and give it to his officers and to his servants. He will take the best of your menservants, your maidservants, your cattle, and your asses and make them work for him. He will take the tenth of your flocks, and you yourselves shall be his slaves. And in that day you will scream and complain about your king whom you wanted; but God will not answer you."

I believe in God, why? I believe in one God, and this God is a man, Jesus. Many say that he is dead. I reply that he is alive. I have a decisive and irrefutable proof. Believing in Jesus living with me, I have a taste for life, and in moments when I forget his presence I no longer live or have any morality. Naturally I choose to live. Jesus, then, is God for me, for with him I can live.

In ch. 8 of the *Philosophy of Misery* I can understand Pierre-Joseph Proudhon very well. He has in view only the one God who is the Supreme Being and who is dominant over us. He could only deny this God, for this God necessarily prevents him from living. He said that if God exists, he is "necessarily hostile to our human nature. Does he really turn out finally to be anything? I do not know that I ever knew him. If I must one day make reconciliation with him, this reconciliation, which is impossible so long as I live, and in which I have everything to gain and nothing to lose, can come about only in my destruction."

The futility of philosophies and theologies. Finally to accept or reject the existence of God is unimportant. What counts is having the taste and joy that life gives. The discussions of philosophers and theologians trying to prove that they are right, and to make out that they are great thinkers, are all futile.

With Paul of Tarsus in 1 Corinthians 3 I maintain that the arguments of the wise are nothing but wind. They are caught in the trap of their own cleverness. Thus a man like Socrates has to die out of respect for the democracy which he thought out.

With John, a friend of Jesus, in 1 John 4, I think that there is nothing we can say about God. No one has ever seen him. We are simply to love one another, for love is of God, and those who love are born of God and know God. Those who do not love have not known God, for God is love. If people say that they love God and hate their brother, they are liars. If wealthy persons see a brother in need and refuse to take pity, how can love be in them?

We believe in Jesus. We acknowledge him as our God and call him God. This is not because we see divine qualities in him: omnipotence, transcendence, eternity, etc. It is because of his attitude of love to others, which leads us to live in the same spirit and gives us a taste for living.

For a revolution — which one? I cannot condemn the oppressed who revolt, take arms, and plunge into violence, but I think that their revolt is ineffective as real revolution. The oppressed will be crushed by those in power, or if they attain to power they will have acquired a taste for power by arms and will thus become new oppressors, so that it will all have to be done over again.

For true revolution we have to find the morality which means acting to remove the source of all violence: the spirit of hierarchy and fear; the fear that rulers have of not being able to live unless they rule, the fear which forces them into violence in order to maintain their rule; the fear also of the ruled that they cannot live unless they overthrow their masters, the fear which impels them to accept the violence which they suffer. The oppressed try to compensate by aiming to rule over others, always at the cost of violence in an infernal cycle of revolt and oppression.

In the spirit of Jesus we fight violence by attacking fear. Jesus says to the oppressed: If someone strikes you on the right cheek, turn the left cheek also. He thus seeks to liberate us from fear of the violence of oppressors. He himself, freed from fear, when he has received a blow does not turn the other cheek but asks for an explanation: "If I have spoken wrongly, show that what I said was wrong; but if I have spoken rightly, why do you strike me?" (John 18:23). He is not afraid of the death to which they are going to subject him.

Jesus also says that if any one takes our coat, we are to give our cloak as well, and if any one makes us go one mile, we are to go two. He wants the oppressed to be freed from the fear of not being able to live without a master. They will then be able to do as he did, treating masters as hypocrites, as a brood of vipers, until they can no longer maintain their spirit of domination (Matthew 23). Masters are always proud of themselves so long as they dominate. We have thus to make them see their baseness and then they will abandon their position, for no people can live when they despise themselves.

Gandhi, Lanza del Vasto, Lech Walesa, and Jesus. It is false to present Gandhi as a champion of nonviolence after the manner of Jesus. Gandhi used nonviolence, but only to establish the oppressive power of the Indian state. He used it against superior British power but he used weapons of war against the weaker. With the leaders of India, his disciples, he sent police against the group which would assassinate him. On Christmas Day he appealed for war against the Sikhs who were demanding independence for the Punjab. His fine thoughts masked the violence which is at the heart of every leader.

Furthermore, the nonviolence of Jesus is very different from that of Lanza del Vasto and more recently that of Lech Walesa. These two fear violence and steer clear of the world of violence. They refuse to attack an oppressive power and thus to bring to light its violence. In 1976 Lanza del Vasto, facing violence, prudently advised us to be gentle and not to respond. Fear of violence led him to accept the violence of nuclear power. We can admire the strong Solidarity movement which Lech Walesa launched in Poland. Unfortunately, he kept the brakes on the movement of liberation. Because those in power threatened violent reaction and bloodshed, he would not allow certain demonstrations. Thus the daily violence of the state continued for many years.

In contrast, Jesus seeks a peace which bypasses conflict and provocation. He realizes that by taking the side of the oppressed he will automatically bring down violence upon himself. He does not shrink, for in his relation with this Father he finds the strength to make his choice. Otherwise he could not live: "the one who would save his life will lose it" (Matthew 16:25).

Not respecting his opponents, Lanza del Vasto refused to denounce their renouncing of all responsibility in obeying the orders of superiors. Jesus, however, treats his enemies in a way which allows them to rediscover their human personality. Lanza del Vasto also lacked respect for the demonstrators. He did not think that they could assume responsibility or evaluate the risks that they were incurring. Jesus, however, warns his friends of the difficulties, shows them what is involved, and lets them make their own choices.

Alvaro Ulcué Chocué and Jesus. In our day I see people merging into the history of those who are animated by a catholic (i.e., universal) spirit, finding brothers and sisters in everyone. Among them there are some who say that they see God in Jesus of Nazareth. They see that he does not pretend to be superior to others but that in love for all he takes the side of the oppressed against oppressors, working to destroy all hierarchy, all power of some over others.

A text published in March 1985 speaks of Alvaro Ulcué Chocué, the only Indian priest in Colombia, who was assassinated in November 1984. His sister had been killed by the police in 1982. Before his death, speaking on one occasion about institutionalized violence, Chocué challenged Christians: "What are we doing? We are watching as spectators and approving by our silence, for we are afraid of proclaiming the gospel in a radical way" (reported Feb. 11, 1985).

The text goes on to say that Christians of the parish of Bozel and Planay, with their priest, having to analyze the situation in the world as it is, reject the violence of states. They have been led to see and denounce the practice of interest rates as the essential cause of violence. One might almost call it a form of assassinating those who are dying of hunger. They denounce especially military budgets and the making and sale of arms. They also oppose the police violence which subjects the poor and opponents to the ruling power, for example, by imprisonment, torture, etc. They call upon their bishops and other Christian communities to join in rejection of this state violence. Hoping for a response, they express to others their union in Jesus.

To strengthen their actions, I believe that Christians and anarchists would do well to get to know one another better.

If libertarians publish this article, it is perhaps because they have a more open spirit than Catholics, whose name really means: "Open to all."

Adrien Duchosal

Conclusion

In writing these pages I have been asking with some anxiety whether anarchist readers will have the patience to read lengthy analyses of biblical texts, whether they will not be wearied or irritated, whether they will see the use, given the fact that they necessarily do not view the Bible as any different from other books or as possibly carrying a Word of God. After all, however, this was part of my subject. And I had to do it well so as to counter fixed ideas of Christianity. This was just as much needed in the case of Christians as of anarchists.

And now, how do I conclude a book of this kind? It seems to me to be important only as a warning to Christians (and as a Christian I have no desire to meddle with anarchist groups). As I see it, what we have learned first is that we must reject totally any Christian spiritualizing, any escape to heaven or the future life (in which I believe, thanks to the resurrection, but which does not sanction any evasion), any mysticism that disdains the things of earth, for God has put us on this earth not for nothing but with a charge that we have no right to refuse. Nevertheless, over against involved

Christians, we have to avoid falling into the trap of the dominant ideology of the day. As I have noted already, the church was monarchist under the kings, imperialist under Napoleon, and republican under the Republic, and now the church (the Protestant Church at least) is becoming socialist in France. This runs contrary to the orientation of Paul, namely, that we are not to be conformed to the ideas of the present world. Here is a first area in which anarchism can form a happy counterweight to the conformist flexibility of Christians. In the ideological and political world, it is a buffer.

Naturally, Christians can hardly be of the right, the actual right, what we have seen the right become. The republican right of the Third Republic had some value.[1] That is not the issue. The right has now become the gross triumph of hypercapitalism or fascism.[2] There is none other. This is ruled out, but so is Marxism in its 20th-century avatars. A Christian cannot be a Stalinist after the Moscow trials, the horrible massacre of anarchists by communists at Barcelona, the German-Soviet pact, the prudent approach of the Communist Party to Maréchalism in 1940, and their conduct after 1944, at the very time when our bold pastors were discovering the beauties of Stalinist communism. Anarchism had seen more clearly and put us on guard. Perhaps we can hear the lesson today.

Finally, anarchism can teach Christian thinkers to see the realities of our societies from a different standpoint than the dominant one of the state. What seems to be one of the disasters of our time is that we all appear to agree that the nation-state is the norm. It is frightening to see that this has

1. Cf. the excellent book by André Tardieu (who was of the right), *Le souverain captif* (1934), in which he denounces the illusory sovereignty of the people.
2. I noted the relation between liberalism and fascism in a long article, "Le Fascisme, fils du libéralisme," *Esprit* 5/53 (Feb. 1, 1937) 761-97.

finally been stronger than the Marxist revolutions, which have all preserved a nationalist structure and state government. It is frightening to think that a desire for secession like that of Makhno was drowned in blood. Whether the state be Marxist or capitalist, it makes no difference. The dominant ideology is that of sovereignty. This makes the construction of a united Europe laughable. No such Europe is possible so long as the states do not renounce their sovereignty. State nationalism has invaded the whole world. Thus all the African peoples, when decolonized, rushed to accept this form. Here is a lesson that anarchism can teach Christians, and it is a very important one.

Need I go on? I said at the outset that I was not trying to Christianize anarchists nor to proclaim an anarchist orientation to be primal for Christians. We must not equate anarchy and Christianity. Nor would I adopt the "same goal" theory which was once used to justify the attachment of Christians to Stalinism. I simply desire it to be stated that there is a general orientation which is common to us both and perfectly clear. This means that we are fighting the same battle from the same standpoint, though with no confusion or illusion. The fact that we face the same adversaries and the same dangers is no little thing. But we also stand by what separates us: on the one side, faith in God and Jesus Christ with all its implications; on the other side, as I have already emphasized, the difference in our evaluation of human nature. I have not pretended to have any other aim or desire in this little essay.

Index of Names

Albigenses, 25, 31
Arles, Synod of, 94-95
Augustus Caesar, 54, 75-76

Barbusse, H., 3
Barth, K., 3, 9, 34-35, 65, 86-88
Basil of Caesarea, 94
Blumhardt, C., 8
Bonner, E., 96
Bookchin, M., 3
Bost, J., 7
Buthelezi, 13

Caesar, Julius, 53, 75
Calvin, J., 45, 79
Cardonnel, P., 56
Castoriadis, C., 22
Cathari, 25, 31
Celsus, 91
Charlemagne, 25
Charrier, Y., 17
Chocué, A. U., 101-2
Chouraqui, A., 34
Constantine, 94

Cromwell, O., 25
Cullmann, O., 83

Dehn, G., 83
Diocletian, 93
Duchosal, A., 96ff.

Eller, V., 3, 8-9, 49
Elvira, Council of, 94

Foucauld, C. de, 7
Fra Dolcino, 7
Francis of Assisi, 7

Gandhi, M., 12, 100
Girard, R., 20

Herod, 53ff.
Herod Antipas, 55
Hippolytus, 93-94
Hitler, A., 29-30, 82, 84
Hornus, J., 91
Hromadka, J., 29

Index of Scripture References

Made in the USA
Middletown, DE
10 October 2014